2023 FACTS & TRIVIA

Snapshot of a Year

David Avera

Published By: Amazon KDP

CONTENTS

INTRODUCTION

2023 was a remarkable year that stood out for several key reasons across various domains:

Pop Culture

2023 saw a resurgence of creativity in the entertainment industry. Blockbuster films and TV series captivated global audiences, with streaming platforms continuing to dominate. Music evolved with new genres blending traditional sounds with modern beats, while social media played a significant role in shaping trends and viral moments. The rise of AI-generated art and music also sparked debates about the future of creativity.

Tech Advancements

2023 was a pivotal year for technology, with significant advancements in artificial intelligence, robotics, and space exploration. AI became more integrated into daily life, with tools like ChatGPT-4 and its successors revolutionizing communication, education, and content creation. Breakthroughs in

quantum computing hinted at a future of unprecedented computational power. Meanwhile, space exploration reached new heights with ambitious missions to Mars and the Moon, reigniting global interest in the final frontier.

Global Events

The world witnessed significant geopolitical shifts in 2023. The year saw major developments in global health, with advancements in vaccine technology and medical treatments. Social movements continued to gain momentum, pushing for equality and justice across various sectors.

Overall, 2023 was a year of transformation and innovation, setting the stage for a dynamic future while reflecting the complexities of our global society.

CHAPTER 1:
Holiday and Cultural Trivia

Unique Holidays and Festivals

1. Great American Beer Festival (United States)

https://www.greatamericanbeerfestival.com/

The **Great American Beer Festival (GABF)** is one of the most prominent and influential beer festivals in the United States, showcasing the diversity and quality of American craft beer. Held annually in Denver, Colorado, the festival attracts thousands of attendees, including beer enthusiasts, industry professionals, and brewers from across the country. Here's a detailed look at what makes the GABF a standout event:

Overview and History

The Great American Beer Festival was first held in 1982 and has grown significantly over the decades. It was founded by the Brewers Association, a non-profit organization that supports small and independent American brewers.

The festival's primary purpose is to celebrate the art of brewing, showcase the range of American craft beers, and provide a platform for breweries to connect with consumers and industry peers. It also aims to promote the craft beer industry and support its growth.

Event Details

Date: The GABF typically takes place over three days in late September or early October. In 2023, the festival was held from September 21-23.

Location: The event is hosted at the Colorado Convention Center in Denver, a venue that provides ample space for the numerous booths and activities associated with the festival.

Attendance: The festival attracts tens of thousands of visitors each year, including beer enthusiasts, brewers, industry professionals, and media representatives. The 2023 event saw a record number of attendees and participating breweries.

Features and Activities

Beer Tastings

The GABF features thousands of craft beers from hundreds of breweries across the U.S. Attendees have the opportunity to sample a wide range of styles, from classic lagers and ales to experimental and seasonal brews.

Both large and small breweries participate, including some of the most well-known names in the craft beer industry as well as up-and-coming and regional brewers.

Competitions and Awards

One of the highlights of the festival is the annual GABF competition, where breweries submit their beers to be judged in various categories. The competition is one of the largest and most prestigious beer competitions in the world.

Winning breweries receive medals in categories such as Best IPA, Best Stout, Best Wheat Beer, and more. These awards are highly coveted and can significantly impact a brewery's reputation and success.

Educational Sessions

The festival offers educational sessions and seminars led by industry experts, covering topics such as brewing techniques, beer styles, and industry trends. These sessions provide valuable insights for both consumers and professionals.

Attendees can also watch live brewing demonstrations and learn about the brewing process from experienced brewers.

Food and Entertainment

The festival features food vendors offering a variety of dishes that complement the beer selections. Food pairings are an integral part of the experience, enhancing the overall enjoyment of the beer.

The GABF includes live music performances and other entertainment options, adding to the festive atmosphere of the event.

Cultural and Economic Impact

Promotion of Craft Beer

The GABF plays a significant role in promoting craft beer and supporting the growth of the industry. It provides exposure for smaller breweries and helps to drive consumer interest in craft beer.

The festival serves as a networking hub for brewers, distributors, and industry professionals, facilitating business relationships and collaborations.

The event provides a substantial economic boost to Denver, with visitors spending on hotels, restaurants, and other local businesses. It also brings attention to the city as a destination for craft beer enthusiasts.

Community Engagement

The Brewers Association and participating breweries often engage in charitable activities and community support. The GABF has been involved in various fundraising efforts and initiatives to benefit local and national causes.

2023 Highlights

The 2023 GABF saw a record number of attendees and participating breweries, reflecting the growing popularity of craft beer and the festival's continued success.

This year's event featured a wide range of innovative and experimental beers, showcasing the creativity and diversity within the craft beer community.

There was a noticeable emphasis on sustainability, with breweries and vendors highlighting eco-friendly practices and products.

The Great American Beer Festival is more than just a celebration of beer; it's a significant cultural event that brings together the craft beer community and enthusiasts from across the nation. With its diverse range of beers, prestigious competitions, educational opportunities, and vibrant atmosphere, the GABF continues to be a cornerstone of the American craft beer scene and a must-attend event for beer lovers and industry professionals alike.

SECHSELÄUTEN (SWITZERLAND)

https://www.sechselaeuten.ch/

Date: April 17, 2023

History and Origins

The origins of Sechseläuten date back to the medieval period when the city's guilds (Zünfte) played a central role in Zurich's social and economic life. In those days, the length of the working day was regulated by daylight, and the ringing of the church bells at six o'clock in the evening signaled the end of the workday. In winter, the bells rang earlier due to shorter days, while in summer, they rang later. The festival symbolizes the transition from the shorter winter workdays to the longer days of summer.

The Parade of Guilds

One of the key features of Sechseläuten is the grand parade that takes place on the festival's main day. Members of Zurich's historic guilds, dressed in traditional costumes, march through the city center, showcasing their heritage. Each guild is accompanied by a marching band, and the participants often ride on horseback or in horse-drawn carriages.

The parade is a colorful and lively affair, with spectators lining the streets to watch the procession. The guilds represent various trades, such as butchers, bakers, blacksmiths, and tailors, and the parade highlights Zurich's rich history and the importance of these trades in the city's development.

Burning of the Böögg

The highlight of Sechseläuten is the burning of the "Böögg," a large snowman effigy stuffed with fireworks. The Böögg, which represents winter, is placed atop a massive bonfire in Sechseläutenplatz, Zurich's central square. As the fire is lit, the crowds eagerly watch to see how long it takes for the Böögg's head to explode.

Trivia: In Zurich, the Sechseläuten festival celebrates the arrival of spring with a parade of guilds and the burning of the "Böögg," a giant snowman effigy. The tradition predicts the coming summer's weather based on how quickly the Böögg's head explodes during the bonfire.

NAADAM FESTIVAL (MONGOLIA)

https://www.visitmongolia.com/

Date: July 11-15, 2023

The Naadam Festival, often referred to as "Eriin Gurvan Naadam" (The Three Manly Games), is Mongolia's largest and most celebrated annual event. It is a vibrant and colorful festival that showcases the nation's rich cultural heritage and deep-rooted traditions. The festival is celebrated nationwide, but the most significant festivities occur in the capital city of Ulaanbaatar.

Historical Background

Naadam's origins trace back over a thousand years, rooted in Mongolia's nomadic culture and the martial traditions of the Mongol Empire. Historically, the festival was a way to test the strength, courage, and skills of warriors, with events that mirrored the military exercises of Genghis Khan's time. Over the centuries, Naadam evolved into a nationwide celebration that includes not only displays of physical prowess but also cultural performances and ceremonies.

The Three Manly Games

The heart of the Naadam Festival is the "Three Manly Games"— wrestling, horse racing, and archery. These sports have been practiced by Mongols for centuries and remain deeply symbolic of Mongolia's nomadic heritage.

Mongolian Wrestling (Bökh)

Wrestling is the most prestigious event of Naadam and holds significant cultural importance. There are no weight classes, meaning smaller wrestlers often compete against much larger opponents, making skill and technique crucial.

The aim is to make the opponent touch the ground with any part of the body other than the feet. Wrestlers wear traditional attire, including a snug-fitting "zodog" (open-front jacket) and "shuudag" (tight shorts). The bouts are single-elimination, and the final winner is awarded the title of "Champion of Naadam."

In 2023, the wrestling competition saw intense matches, with a mix of seasoned champions and new contenders. The final bout was particularly memorable, drawing large crowds and national attention.

Horse Racing (Morin Khuur)

Mongolian horse racing is unlike the shorter, track-based races seen in other parts of the world. In Naadam, races are long-distance, often covering 15 to 30 kilometers (9 to 18 miles), depending on the age category of the horses.

Riders are typically young children, some as young as five years old, who have been trained to ride horses from a very young age. The focus is on the horses' speed and endurance, rather than just the riders' skills.

The 2023 races featured over 1,000 horses competing in various categories. A particularly young rider captured the nation's heart, finishing first in the two-year-old horse category, showcasing the next generation of Mongolia's equestrian tradition.

Archery (Sur Kharvaa)

Archery is another ancient sport celebrated during Naadam, with both men and women participating. Mongolian archery differs from Western styles, with archers shooting arrows at small, leather rings or cylindrical targets placed at varying distances.

Traditional bows made from sinew, wood, and horn are used, reflecting centuries-old craftsmanship. The targets are positioned between 65 and 75 meters away for men, and between 55 and 65 meters for women.

In 2023, the archery competition saw a record number of participants, with many competitors showcasing remarkable accuracy. The event highlighted the enduring popularity and cultural significance of archery in Mongolia.

Cultural Significance and Ceremonies

Naadam is not just about sports; it is also a time of national pride, cultural expression, and community celebration. The festival begins with an elaborate opening ceremony in Ulaanbaatar, featuring performances by dancers, musicians, and singers. The ceremony includes a parade of athletes, traditional Mongolian attire, and a reenactment of historical events, such as Genghis Khan's conquests.

The festival also has deep spiritual significance, with rituals and offerings made to the spirits of the land, horses, and ancestors. The event is closely tied to Mongolia's shamanistic and Buddhist traditions, blending the country's spiritual and secular worlds.

Naadam 2023: A Memorable Year

In 2023, Naadam marked a significant milestone as it was the first full-scale celebration following the COVID-19 pandemic. The festival saw a resurgence in participation and spectatorship, with many people attending in person after years of limited gatherings. The government and local organizers made significant efforts to preserve the authenticity of the festival while also incorporating modern elements, such as live streaming and digital outreach, allowing a global audience to experience Naadam.

Naadam 2023 also included a focus on environmental conservation, with initiatives to reduce waste and promote sustainable practices during the festivities. This was in line with Mongolia's broader efforts to protect its unique ecosystems and cultural heritage.

The Legacy of Naadam

The Naadam Festival is more than just a sporting event; it is a celebration of Mongolia's national identity, history, and community spirit. It serves as a reminder of the country's nomadic roots and the enduring legacy of its ancient traditions. Each year, Naadam brings together Mongolians from all walks of life to honor their shared heritage and look forward to the future.

Whether through the thunder of hooves in the horse races, the strength and skill of the wrestlers, or the precision of the archers, Naadam continues to be a powerful symbol of Mongolian culture and pride.

Trivia: Naadam is Mongolia's biggest celebration, featuring the "Three Manly Games" of wrestling, horse racing, and archery. In 2023, the festival celebrated its 102nd anniversary since becoming a national holiday, attracting visitors from around the world to witness these traditional sports.

GION MATSURI (JAPAN)

https://www.kyototourism.org/

Date: July 1-31, 2023

Gion Matsuri is one of Japan's most famous and vibrant festivals, held annually in Kyoto throughout the month of July. This festival is not only a showcase of traditional Japanese culture but also a reflection of Kyoto's rich history and deep spiritual heritage. Gion Matsuri dates back over a thousand years and is celebrated with a series of events, including grand parades, intricate rituals, and community gatherings.

Historical Background

Gion Matsuri originated in 869 AD during the Heian period as a religious ceremony to appease the gods and ward off plagues that were devastating Kyoto at the time. The festival was organized by the citizens of Kyoto to pray to the deity of Yasaka Shrine, which is closely associated with the Gion district of the city.

Originally, portable shrines (mikoshi) were carried through the streets to purify the city and protect it from epidemics. Over time, the festival evolved, incorporating elements of local culture, arts, and community participation, becoming one of Japan's most important cultural events.

Key Events of Gion Matsuri

Gion Matsuri is a month-long festival, with the highlights being the grand processions known as the **Yamaboko Junko**. These processions take place on July 17th (Saki Matsuri) and July 24th

(Ato Matsuri), and they are the most iconic and visually stunning aspects of the festival.

Yamaboko Junko

The Yamaboko Junko parades feature two types of floats: the massive, wheeled "hoko" floats, which can be up to 25 meters tall and weigh around 12 tons, and the smaller, more agile "yama" floats. Each float is richly decorated with tapestries, lanterns, and carvings, often representing stories from Japanese mythology or historical events.

The floats are constructed without using nails; instead, they are held together by ropes and wooden joints, showcasing traditional Japanese craftsmanship. The assembly of the floats is a significant event in itself, with local communities coming together to build and decorate them.

On the day of the parade, the floats are pulled through the streets of Kyoto by teams of men in traditional attire, accompanied by musicians playing traditional instruments like flutes and drums. The procession moves slowly, allowing spectators to appreciate the intricate details of the floats. Each float is also accompanied by a group of local children dressed in traditional costumes, who play an important role in the ceremonies.

Yoiyama Evenings

In the days leading up to the Yamaboko Junko parades, the Yoiyama evenings (July 14-16 for Saki Matsuri and July 21-23 for Ato Matsuri) are held. During these nights, the streets of Kyoto's downtown are pedestrianized and lined with food stalls, games, and souvenir stands. The festival atmosphere is lively, with locals and visitors wearing summer yukata (light cotton kimono) and enjoying traditional street food.

The Yamaboko floats are stationed in the streets, illuminated by lanterns, and open to the public for viewing. Some of the floats also offer access to the top, where visitors can see the city from a unique perspective. During these evenings, many families open their homes to display treasured family heirlooms, creating an atmosphere of community and shared culture.

Mikoshi Procession

Another significant event during Gion Matsuri is the Mikoshi procession, where portable shrines (mikoshi) are carried through the streets. These mikoshi are believed to carry the spirits of the deities from Yasaka Shrine, who are taken on a tour of the city to bless the people and ensure their protection.

The procession is divided into two parts: the initial departure on July 17th and the return on July 24th. During the return, the deities are brought back to Yasaka Shrine, concluding the festival's major events.

Cultural and Spiritual Significance

Gion Matsuri is deeply rooted in Shinto beliefs and practices. The festival is seen as a way to purify the city and its inhabitants, ensuring a year of good health and prosperity. The rituals, prayers, and offerings made during the festival are central to its spiritual purpose.

The floats themselves are not just decorative; they are considered sacred, and the construction and parading of the floats are acts of devotion. Each float represents a specific neighborhood or community in Kyoto, and participating in the festival is a matter of great pride for the residents.

Gion Matsuri in 2023

The 2023 Gion Matsuri was particularly significant as it marked the full return of all festival events after the disruptions caused by the COVID-19 pandemic in previous years. The city of Kyoto saw a large influx of visitors, both domestic and international, eager to experience the festival in its full glory.

In 2023, special emphasis was placed on preserving traditional practices while also incorporating modern elements to appeal to younger generations. For instance, digital guides and augmented reality experiences were introduced to enhance the understanding and appreciation of the festival's rich history.

Gion Matsuri Today

Today, Gion Matsuri is not only a religious and cultural festival but also a major tourist attraction. It draws people from all over the world to Kyoto, offering a unique opportunity to experience traditional Japanese culture up close. The festival's blend of spiritual significance, artistic expression, and community involvement continues to make it a highlight of the Japanese calendar.

The Gion Matsuri remains a testament to Kyoto's enduring legacy as the cultural heart of Japan, where ancient traditions are kept alive and celebrated with the same fervor and respect as they were centuries ago.

Trivia: This month-long festival in Kyoto is one of Japan's most famous, but its specific rituals and events remain lesser-known outside the country. In 2023, the Gion Matsuri featured elaborate floats called "yamaboko" and a unique purification ceremony known as "Chinowa Kuguri," where participants walk through a large ring made of grass to ward off misfortune.

CHINCHILLA MELON FESTIVAL (AUSTRALIA)

http://www.melonfestival.com.au/

Date: February 16-19, 2023

The Chinchilla Melon Festival, held in Chinchilla, Queensland, Australia, is a unique and quirky celebration dedicated to one of the region's most famous agricultural products: the watermelon. Known as the "Melon Capital of Australia," Chinchilla hosts this biennial event, drawing thousands of visitors to enjoy a variety of melon-themed activities and competitions. The festival is a testament to the town's vibrant community spirit and agricultural heritage.

History and Origins

The Chinchilla Melon Festival began in 1994 as a way to boost local morale and tourism during a period of economic downturn caused by severe drought. The event was initially conceived as a fun, family-friendly gathering to celebrate the town's significant melon farming industry, which has long been a vital part of the local economy.

Chinchilla's fertile soil and favorable climate make it ideal for growing watermelons, rockmelons (cantaloupes), and honeydew melons. Over the years, the Melon Festival has grown in popularity, becoming one of Australia's most iconic regional festivals, known for its unique and sometimes wacky events centered around melons.

Festival Highlights

The Chinchilla Melon Festival is a four-day event filled with a wide range of activities and competitions, many of which are centered around melons. The festival is as much about having fun as it is about celebrating the town's agricultural success.

Melon Skiing

Perhaps the most famous and eye-catching event of the festival is melon skiing. Participants strap watermelons to their feet and attempt to "ski" down a slick, soapy plastic track. The challenge is to stay upright as long as possible, with many participants ending up hilariously slipping and sliding across the track. Melon skiing has become a symbol of the festival, capturing the imagination of attendees and often being featured in media coverage of the event.

Melon Bungee

In this event, participants are tethered to a bungee cord and must race as far as they can while carrying a large watermelon before being snapped back by the cord. It's a test of strength, speed, and balance, and often ends with participants tumbling into the grass, much to the delight of onlookers. The melon bungee is both a crowd-pleaser and a test of agility and endurance, with participants competing for the longest distance covered.

Melon Chariot Races

Teams construct chariots made from melon crates and other materials, and then race them in a relay-style competition. The chariots are often creatively decorated, adding to the festive atmosphere. The race requires both speed and teamwork, making it a favorite among participants. The chariot races highlight the community spirit of the festival, with teams often including local businesses, families, and friends competing in a good-natured rivalry.

Melon Toss

The melon toss is a simple yet entertaining event where participants throw a watermelon as far as they can. The competition is divided into different age categories, allowing both children and adults to participate. Over the years, the melon toss has seen some impressive distances, with participants striving to set new records.

Melon Dash

The Melon Dash is a race where participants carry a large watermelon over a set distance. The challenge lies in the weight and awkward shape of the melon, making it difficult to run quickly without dropping it. This race is a highlight for many festival-goers, with locals and visitors alike taking part in the fun.

Additional Events and Activities

In addition to the signature melon-themed competitions, the Chinchilla Melon Festival features a variety of other events, including:

A colorful parade that showcases floats, marching bands, and performers, celebrating the town's heritage and community. The festival includes live performances by local and national musicians, as well as other forms of entertainment such as comedy shows and dance performances. While melons take center stage, the festival also features a wide array of food vendors offering everything from traditional Australian cuisine to international dishes. Of course, there are plenty of melon-based treats, including fresh slices, juices, and even melon-flavored ice cream.

Local artisans and vendors set up stalls selling crafts, clothing, and other goods, giving visitors a chance to purchase unique souvenirs and support local businesses. For those who prefer to enjoy melons the traditional way, there are competitive eating contests where participants race to devour as much watermelon as possible in a limited time.

Chinchilla Melon Festival 2023

The 2023 Chinchilla Melon Festival was particularly special, as it marked a return to full-scale celebrations after the disruptions caused by the COVID-19 pandemic. The event attracted a record number of visitors, with many eager to partake in the fun and unique activities that the festival is known for.

This year, the festival also focused on sustainability, with efforts to reduce waste and promote environmentally friendly practices. Organizers introduced initiatives such as composting melon rinds and using biodegradable materials for food packaging.

In 2023, the festival also featured special guest appearances, including Australian celebrities who participated in some of the melon-themed events, further boosting the festival's profile and adding to the excitement.

Cultural and Economic Impact

The Chinchilla Melon Festival plays a significant role in promoting the town of Chinchilla and its agricultural heritage. The festival brings together locals and visitors, fostering a sense of community and pride. It also provides a substantial economic boost to the region, with local businesses benefiting from the influx of tourists.

For many visitors, the festival is a chance to experience rural Australian culture and participate in events that are distinctly unique to this part of the world. The festival has become a key part of Chinchilla's identity, drawing attention to the town and its agricultural achievements.

The Chinchilla Melon Festival is a fun, quirky, and uniquely Australian celebration that perfectly captures the spirit of the local community. With its melon-themed events, vibrant atmosphere, and emphasis on fun for all ages, the festival offers something for everyone. Whether you're melon skiing, tossing, or just enjoying a slice of fresh watermelon, the Chinchilla Melon Festival is an unforgettable experience that celebrates the simple joy of summer and the importance of community.

Trivia: Held biennially in Chinchilla, Queensland, this quirky festival celebrates the region's melon farming heritage. The 2023 event included unusual competitions like melon skiing, melon bungee jumping, and the "Melon Dash," where participants race while carrying heavy watermelons.

THAIPUSAM (MALAYSIA)

http://www.batucavestemple.com.my/
https://www.penangtourism.com/

Date: February 5, 2023

Thaipusam is a significant Hindu festival observed primarily by the Tamil community in India, Sri Lanka, Malaysia, Singapore, and various other countries with Tamil diaspora. The festival is dedicated to Lord Murugan, the Hindu god of war and victory, who is also known as Kartikeya or Subramanya. Thaipusam is celebrated with great fervor and devotion, marked by elaborate rituals, vibrant processions, and acts of penance.

Origins and Significance

The name "Thaipusam" is derived from the Tamil month of "Thai" (January-February) and the star "Pusam" (Pushya), which is at its highest point during the festival. According to Hindu mythology, Thaipusam commemorates the day when Parvati, the mother of Murugan, gave him a divine spear (Vel) to defeat the demon Soorapadman and restore peace and righteousness.

Thaipusam symbolizes the triumph of good over evil, and it is a time for devotees to seek blessings, fulfill vows, and perform acts of penance as a demonstration of their faith and devotion. The festival is particularly associated with self-purification, spiritual renewal, and the expiation of sins.

Rituals and Practices

Thaipusam is marked by a series of rituals that vary in intensity and significance, depending on the level of devotion. The following are some of the key practices observed during the festival:

Kavadi Attam (Burden Dance)

The central ritual of Thaipusam is the carrying of the **kavadi**, a physical burden that devotees take on as an act of devotion and penance. The kavadi is usually a semi-circular, decorated structure that is carried on the shoulders. It can range from simple, small structures to elaborate, towering ones adorned with flowers, peacock feathers, and other decorations.

The kavadi can be of various types, with some devotees carrying pots of milk (Paal Kudam) or other offerings, while others may undertake more extreme forms of penance by piercing their bodies with skewers and hooks.

In a display of extreme devotion, some participants pierce their tongues, cheeks, or other parts of their bodies with sharp objects, often attached to the kavadi. These acts of self-mortification are believed to help devotees attain spiritual purification and fulfill vows made to Lord Murugan.

Vow Fulfillment

Many devotees undertake specific vows (vratams) in the lead-up to Thaipusam, such as fasting, maintaining celibacy, and adhering to a vegetarian diet. These vows are usually made in gratitude for blessings received or as a form of penance for sins committed.

Before carrying the kavadi, devotees undergo ritual purification, which includes bathing, prayer, and meditation. This purification process is essential to prepare the mind and body for the physical and spiritual challenges of the kavadi ritual.

Processions

Thaipusam is characterized by grand processions in which devotees, often barefoot, carry the kavadi from one temple to another. The most famous processions take place in Malaysia, particularly at the Batu Caves near Kuala Lumpur, and in Singapore at the Sri Thendayuthapani Temple.

The Batu Caves procession is one of the most iconic Thaipusam events. Devotees walk several kilometers to reach the caves, ascending 272 steps to the temple at the top. The atmosphere is charged with spiritual fervor, with the air filled with the sound of traditional music, chanting, and prayers.

The processions are attended by large crowds, including both participants and onlookers. Families, friends, and fellow devotees provide support, offering water, food, and encouragement to those carrying the kavadi.

Thaipusam in 2023

Thaipusam in 2023 saw a significant return to traditional celebrations after the restrictions of the COVID-19 pandemic in previous years. Devotees across the world participated in the festival with renewed enthusiasm and devotion.

The Batu Caves in Malaysia, a focal point of Thaipusam celebrations, witnessed a large turnout of devotees and tourists. The festival was celebrated with the usual grandeur, and the procession to the caves was marked by the presence of numerous kavadi bearers performing acts of penance.

In Singapore, the procession from the Sri Srinivasa Perumal Temple to the Sri Thendayuthapani Temple attracted thousands of participants. The event was well-organized, with authorities ensuring the safety and well-being of all attendees while maintaining the spiritual sanctity of the occasion.

In Tamil Nadu, the festival was observed with devotion at major Murugan temples such as the Arulmigu Dhandayuthapani

Swamy Temple in Palani, where a significant number of devotees gathered to offer prayers and fulfill vows.

Cultural and Spiritual Impact

Thaipusam is not only a religious festival but also a profound expression of cultural identity for the Tamil community. It serves as a reminder of the enduring power of faith and the ability of individuals to overcome physical and mental challenges through devotion and discipline.

The festival also fosters a strong sense of community, as families, friends, and even strangers come together to support one another in fulfilling their vows. The collective experience of participating in or witnessing the rituals of Thaipusam creates a deep bond among those who share the same faith and cultural heritage.

Modern Perspectives

In recent years, Thaipusam has also attracted attention from non-Hindus and tourists, who are drawn to the festival's unique and intense rituals. While some view the extreme forms of penance with fascination, others are inspired by the spiritual commitment displayed by the devotees. However, the growing popularity of Thaipusam has also led to discussions about maintaining the sanctity and authenticity of the festival. Efforts are being made to ensure that the festival remains a genuine expression of faith, rather than merely a spectacle for onlookers.

Thaipusam is a deeply spiritual and culturally rich festival that highlights the devotion and resilience of the Tamil Hindu community. It is a time of intense prayer, penance, and gratitude, where devotees push the limits of their physical and spiritual endurance to honor Lord Murugan. The festival's vibrant processions, colorful rituals, and acts of extreme devotion make Thaipusam one of the most remarkable and revered celebrations in the Hindu calendar.

Trivia: Thaipusam is a Hindu festival celebrated primarily in Malaysia, Singapore, and India. Devotees perform acts of penance, including carrying "kavadi" (burdens) and piercing their bodies with hooks and spears. In 2023, the event drew large crowds to Batu Caves near Kuala Lumpur, where a massive procession took place.

BURNING OF THE CLOCKS (UK)

https://www.burningoftheclocks.co.uk/

Date: December 21, 2023

The Burning of the Clocks is a unique and enchanting winter solstice festival held annually in Brighton, UK. This event, which combines elements of art, community, and tradition, marks the shortest day of the year and serves as a symbolic farewell to the old year while welcoming the new. Unlike many other festivals, the Burning of the Clocks is a contemporary creation, yet it has quickly become a beloved and integral part of Brighton's cultural calendar.

Origins and Concept

The Burning of the Clocks was first introduced in 1993 by Same Sky, a community arts charity based in Brighton. The festival was conceived as a way to bring people together during the winter season, offering an inclusive celebration that transcends religious affiliations and cultural backgrounds. It was designed to be a non-commercial, community-driven event that emphasizes creativity, participation, and the collective spirit of the city.

The festival's name and concept revolve around the theme of time, symbolized by clocks. It reflects the passage of time and the transition from one year to the next, with the burning of lanterns representing the release of the past and the anticipation of the future.

Festival Highlights

The Burning of the Clocks is known for its distinctive combination of art, performance, and communal participation. The key elements of the festival include the lantern-making workshops, the lantern procession, and the culminating bonfire on Brighton's beach.

Lantern-Making Workshops

In the weeks leading up to the festival, community members are invited to participate in lantern-making workshops organized by Same Sky. These workshops are open to people of all ages and encourage participants to create their own unique lanterns, often incorporating symbols, shapes, and designs that hold personal significance.

The lanterns are made from biodegradable materials, such as willow and tissue paper, and are designed to be lightweight and easy to carry. Many of the lanterns take the shape of clocks or other time-related symbols, aligning with the festival's theme. The process of making the lanterns is as much a part of the celebration as the procession itself, fostering creativity and a sense of community.

Lantern Procession

On the evening of the winter solstice, participants gather in central Brighton to take part in a stunning lantern procession. The procession winds its way through the streets of the city, with participants carrying their illuminated lanterns and accompanied by music, drummers, and performers. The sight of hundreds of glowing lanterns moving through the dark streets creates a magical and otherworldly atmosphere.

The procession is open to everyone, regardless of background or belief. It's a time for the community to come together in a shared experience of light and celebration. Participants often dress in costumes or wear simple, dark clothing that allows the lanterns to be the focal point.

The Bonfire and Burning of the Clocks

The procession culminates at Brighton's seafront, where a large bonfire is built on the beach. The bonfire serves as the centerpiece of the evening's finale. As the participants arrive at the beach, they place their lanterns into the bonfire, symbolically releasing the burdens and memories of the past year.

The act of burning the lanterns is deeply symbolic, representing the passage of time and the transition from one year to the next. The fire, which consumes the lanterns and illuminates the night sky, is a powerful visual metaphor for renewal and the cyclical nature of time. The event typically ends with a fireworks display, adding a celebratory and triumphant note to the evening.

Cultural and Community Impact

The Burning of the Clocks has become a cherished tradition in Brighton, drawing both local residents and visitors to participate in this unique celebration. It is a festival that emphasizes community, creativity, and inclusivity, offering a shared space for reflection and renewal at the close of the year.

One of the defining characteristics of the Burning of the Clocks is its non-commercial ethos. The festival is not associated with any particular religious or commercial agenda, making it accessible and appealing to a broad audience. The focus is on participation and the communal experience, rather than on consumption or profit.

The festival provides a platform for artistic expression, both for professional artists and for community members. The lanterns themselves are works of art, each one reflecting the creativity and individuality of its maker. The festival also includes performances by local musicians, dancers, and street performers, further enhancing its cultural significance.

Burning of the Clocks in 2023

The 2023 Burning of the Clocks was particularly poignant, as it marked a full return to the traditional format after the challenges posed by the COVID-19 pandemic in previous years. The event saw a high level of participation, with many people eager to reconnect with this beloved community tradition.

In 2023, the theme of the festival was "Resilience," reflecting the collective experiences of the community over the past few years. Participants were encouraged to design their lanterns with symbols of strength, endurance, and hope, creating a powerful visual narrative during the procession.

Environmental Considerations

Given its focus on community and sustainability, the Burning of the Clocks has increasingly emphasized environmental responsibility. The lanterns are made from biodegradable materials, and the festival organizers have taken steps to ensure that the event leaves a minimal environmental footprint. This includes careful management of the bonfire and a commitment to cleaning up the beach after the event.

The Burning of the Clocks is a truly unique festival that encapsulates the spirit of Brighton. It is a celebration of time, community, and creativity, offering a space for reflection and renewal as the year comes to a close. The festival's blend of art, ritual, and communal participation makes it one of the most distinctive and meaningful events in the UK's cultural calendar, drawing people together in a shared experience of light, warmth, and the enduring passage of time.

Trivia: This unique winter solstice event in Brighton, England, combines art and community spirit. Participants create paper lanterns representing clocks, symbolizing the passing of time, and then parade through the streets before burning the lanterns in a beach bonfire. The 2023 celebration was particularly poignant as it marked the event's 30th anniversary.

LA TOMATINA DE BUÑOL (SPAIN)

https://www.latomatina.org/
https://www.bunol.es/

Date: August 30, 2023

La Tomatina de Buñol is one of the most famous and unique festivals in Spain, attracting thousands of participants from around the world. Held annually on the last Wednesday of August in the small town of Buñol, located in the Valencia region, this vibrant and chaotic event is essentially a massive tomato fight. It has become a symbol of Spanish fun and exuberance, showcasing the country's love for festivals and community gatherings.

History and Origins

The origins of La Tomatina are somewhat obscure, with various stories and legends surrounding its inception. The most widely accepted version dates back to 1945. According to local lore, during a parade of gigantes y cabezudos (giant figures with big heads) in Buñol, a group of young people attempted to join in the parade, causing one participant to fall. In retaliation, the person started throwing vegetables at the crowd, leading to a spontaneous food fight. The following year, the same group of young people returned to the town square with tomatoes, and thus, La Tomatina was born.

The festival was not initially an official event and was even banned several times during its early years. However, the persistence of locals kept the tradition alive, and in 1957, after a ceremonial "funeral" for the tomato fight was held to protest its banning, the town council relented and officially recognized the event. Since then, La Tomatina has grown in popularity, becoming an internationally recognized festival.

The Festival Today

La Tomatina has evolved into a major tourist attraction, drawing participants from all over the globe. Despite its humble beginnings, the festival now requires tickets for participation to control the crowd size, with only about 20,000 participants allowed to join in the fun each year.

Festival Preparation

The tomatoes used in La Tomatina are specifically grown for the event and are not fit for consumption. They are generally low-quality, overripe, and relatively soft, ensuring that they cause no harm when thrown. The town orders around 150,000 tomatoes, which equates to over 40 metric tons.

On the morning of La Tomatina, trucks loaded with tomatoes make their way to the town's main square, Plaza del Pueblo. Streets are lined with protective plastic coverings, and participants are advised to wear old clothes and goggles to protect their eyes from the acidic juice.

The Event Itself

The festivities begin around 10 a.m. with a tradition known as "Palo Jabón," where participants attempt to climb a greased pole to reach a ham placed at the top. Once someone successfully retrieves the ham, a cannon is fired to signal the start of the tomato fight.

As soon as the cannon sounds, the trucks unload their cargo of tomatoes, and the crowd goes wild. For about an hour, participants hurl tomatoes at each other in what becomes a sea of red pulp. The only rule is to squash the tomatoes before throwing them to minimize the risk of injury.

After an hour, the second cannon blast signals the end of the fight. The streets of Buñol are left covered in tomato puree, and participants are drenched in red juice. Locals and fire trucks then wash down the streets, while participants clean themselves off at nearby public showers or in the Buñol River.

Cultural and Social Impact

La Tomatina is more than just a tomato fight; it is a reflection of the Spanish spirit of celebration, community, and joy. The festival's success has also turned it into a significant economic driver for Buñol, attracting tourists who spend money on accommodation, food, and other local services.

The festival's uniqueness and fun nature have given it global appeal, with people traveling from various countries to experience the event. It has also inspired similar events in other parts of the world, though none quite match the scale or authenticity of the original.

La Tomatina has been featured in numerous travel shows, documentaries, and even in films, further solidifying its place as one of Spain's most iconic festivals.

Environmental Considerations

Given the massive amount of tomatoes used, environmental concerns have been raised over the years. However, the tomatoes used are of low commercial value and are specifically grown for the event. Additionally, the town takes measures to ensure that the cleanup is efficient and environmentally friendly. The acidic nature of the tomato juice actually has a cleansing effect on the streets, leaving them cleaner than before.

La Tomatina in 2023

The 2023 edition of La Tomatina saw a full return to its pre-pandemic scale, with a vibrant turnout of participants eager to engage in the world's biggest food fight. The event was marked by the usual chaos and camaraderie, with people from diverse backgrounds coming together for a day of unbridled fun.

The festival also featured side events such as music performances, parades, and local food tastings, making it a comprehensive cultural experience. The presence of international media and social media influencers further amplified the festival's global reach, drawing attention from new audiences.

La Tomatina de Buñol is a festival that perfectly encapsulates the joyous and irreverent spirit of Spanish culture. Its blend of tradition, spontaneity, and communal fun has made it an event like no other, attracting people from around the world to a small town in Valencia every August. Whether you're a participant or a spectator, La Tomatina offers an unforgettable experience filled with laughter, mess, and the simple pleasure of letting go and embracing the chaos.

Trivia: While La Tomatina is widely known, the cultural significance behind this massive tomato fight is less familiar. It began in 1945 as a spontaneous food fight during a parade. In 2023, around 22,000 participants gathered in Buñol to hurl over 145,000 kg of tomatoes at each other, turning the streets into a sea of red.

WALPURGIS NIGHT (SWEDEN)

https://visitsweden.com/

Date: April 30, 2023

Walpurgis Night, known as **Walpurgisnacht** in German, is a traditional European festival celebrated on the night of April 30th, leading into May 1st. It is particularly popular in Germany, Sweden, Finland, the Czech Republic, and Estonia. The festival is named after **Saint Walpurga**, an 8th-century abbess in Francia, who was canonized on May 1st, and her feast day was associated with the festival. Over time, Walpurgis Night has evolved into a blend of Christian and pagan traditions, marked by bonfires, celebrations, and a certain air of mysticism.

Origins and Historical Background

Walpurgis Night has its roots in both pagan and Christian traditions. The celebration originally coincided with the pagan festival of **Beltane**, which marked the beginning of summer and was associated with fertility, protection, and the warding off of evil spirits. The Celts and Germanic tribes would light bonfires to ward off witches and evil spirits and to ensure a good harvest.

With the spread of Christianity, the festival was integrated into the Christian calendar, and Saint Walpurga, who was invoked for protection against witchcraft and evil spirits, became associated with the night. Over time, the festival retained its magical and protective elements, even as it took on new Christian meanings.

Walpurgis Night Traditions

Walpurgis Night is celebrated with various customs and traditions that vary from region to region. However, some common themes include bonfires, the warding off of witches, and the welcoming of spring.

Bonfires

The central element of Walpurgis Night is the lighting of bonfires, which are believed to have protective properties. The flames are thought to ward off evil spirits, witches, and other malevolent forces that are believed to be particularly active on this night.

In many regions, communities come together to build large bonfires, often on hilltops or in open fields. These gatherings are festive occasions, with singing, dancing, and the sharing of food and drink. The bonfire is a symbol of purification and protection, as well as a means of celebrating the arrival of spring.

Witches and Magic

Walpurgis Night is steeped in folklore, particularly in Germany and the surrounding regions. It was traditionally believed that witches gathered on this night on the Brocken, the highest peak of the Harz Mountains, to hold a wild feast and to meet with the devil. The image of witches flying on broomsticks to their secret gatherings is a common motif associated with the night.

To protect themselves from witches and evil spirits, people would hang crosses, herbs, and other protective items on their doors and windows. Loud noises, such as the ringing of church bells or the banging of drums, were also used to scare away malevolent forces.

Maypole and Spring Celebrations

In some regions, Walpurgis Night merges with May Day celebrations, which include the raising of the maypole (a tall pole decorated with ribbons and flowers) and maypole dancing. The maypole is a symbol of fertility and the renewal of life, and the dancing around it is a way of welcoming the new season.

Walpurgis Night also marks the end of winter and the beginning of spring. In many places, people dress in white to symbolize purity and the return of light after the dark winter months. The night is filled with singing and dancing, celebrating the rebirth of nature.

Modern Celebrations

In Germany, particularly in the Harz Mountains, Walpurgis Night is celebrated with elaborate festivals, including costumed parades, theatrical performances, and music. Towns like Wernigerode and Thale are known for their large-scale Walpurgis Night events, where thousands of people gather to enjoy the festivities.

In Sweden, Walpurgis Night, or **Valborgsmässsoafton**, is one of the most popular traditional festivals. It is celebrated with large bonfires, choral singing, and speeches, often organized by universities and student organizations. The celebration is particularly significant in Uppsala and Lund, where students play a central role in the festivities.

In Finland, the night is known as **Vappu**, and it is a major celebration, especially among students. The event includes the crowning of the Havis Amanda statue in Helsinki, parades, and the wearing of student caps. Vappu is also associated with labor day celebrations and is marked by large public gatherings, picnics, and the consumption of traditional foods and drinks, such as mead and funnel cakes.

Walpurgis Night in 2023

The 2023 celebrations of Walpurgis Night saw a resurgence in traditional festivities after the disruptions caused by the COVID-19 pandemic in previous years. Many towns and cities across Europe held large public events, attracting both locals and tourists eager to experience the cultural richness of the festival.

In Germany, the Harz Mountains were once again the focal point of Walpurgis Night activities. Events included historical reenactments of witch trials, fire dances, and medieval markets, all contributing to the atmosphere of mysticism and folklore.

Swedish cities like Uppsala and Lund saw massive gatherings of students and locals, with the traditional bonfires and choral singing making a strong comeback. The festival was also marked by a renewed interest in sustainability, with organizers encouraging eco-friendly practices during the celebrations.

Cultural Significance

Walpurgis Night holds a special place in European cultural heritage, blending pagan, Christian, and local traditions into a night of celebration and mystery. It reflects the enduring human need to mark the changing seasons, to protect against the unknown, and to celebrate life in community.

While the more fantastical elements of Walpurgis Night, such as witch gatherings, are rooted in myth, they reflect historical fears and beliefs about the supernatural. The festival provides a way for modern people to connect with these ancient traditions in a playful and symbolic manner.

At its heart, Walpurgis Night is about community—whether through the shared experience of a bonfire, the collective effort of raising a maypole, or the communal joy of singing and dancing. It's a time for people to come together, to celebrate the end of winter, and to look forward to the warmth and growth of spring.

Walpurgis Night is a festival that beautifully encapsulates the intersection of history, myth, and communal celebration. Whether observed as a night of magical traditions, a celebration of spring, or simply a time for community gathering, it remains a vibrant and cherished part of the cultural fabric in many parts of Europe. The festival's combination of bonfires, folklore, and revelry continues to attract both participants and spectators, making it a night of light, laughter, and a touch of magic.

Trivia: Known as "Valborg" in Sweden, Walpurgis Night celebrates the arrival of spring with bonfires and singing. In 2023, cities across Sweden, especially Uppsala and Lund, hosted large gatherings where people sang traditional spring songs, danced, and enjoyed fireworks.

CHAPTER 2:

Tech & Innovations

2023's Coolest Gadgets

2023 was an exciting year for technology, with numerous innovative gadgets hitting the market. These devices spanned various categories, from smartphones and wearable tech to smart home devices and health gadgets, each pushing the boundaries of what technology can do. Here's a look at some of the most innovative gadgets released in 2023:

APPLE VISION PRO

https://www.apple.com/apple-vision-pro

The **Apple Vision Pro**, released in 2023, is Apple's groundbreaking entry into the world of augmented reality (AR) and mixed reality (MR). The device represents a significant leap forward in immersive technology, blending digital content with the physical world in a seamless and intuitive way. Here's an in-depth look at what makes the Apple Vision Pro such an innovative and influential device:

Design and Build

The Apple Vision Pro features a sleek, modern design with a focus on comfort and wearability. It's built with high-quality materials, including a lightweight aluminum frame and a soft, adjustable headband that ensures a secure fit for various head sizes. The front of the device includes a curved, seamless glass visor that houses an array of sensors and cameras. The visor not only looks futuristic but also contributes to the immersive experience by offering a wide field of view.

Display Technology

The Vision Pro is equipped with advanced micro-OLED displays that deliver incredibly sharp and vibrant visuals. Each display boasts a resolution that far exceeds what's available in most other AR and VR headsets, offering a stunning level of detail and clarity. The headset provides a wide field of view, allowing users to see a broad expanse of digital content overlaid on the real world. This wide view helps create a more natural and immersive experience.

Augmented Reality Experience

Apple Vision Pro's AR capabilities are designed to seamlessly blend digital content with the physical environment. This means users can see and interact with digital objects as if they were part of the real world. For example, you might see virtual screens floating in your living room, or digital artwork displayed on your walls. The device allows for complex interactions with digital content. Users can use hand gestures, voice commands, and eye tracking to control and manipulate AR elements. This intuitive control scheme makes the device accessible even to those unfamiliar with AR technology.

The Vision Pro is packed with sensors that track the user's movements, gestures, and surroundings with high precision. These include LiDAR sensors, which map the physical environment in 3D, and a range of cameras that capture the user's surroundings in real-time. The device features sophisticated eye-tracking technology, allowing users to select and interact with objects simply by looking at them. This feature significantly enhances the user experience by making interactions faster and more intuitive.

Performance and Hardware

The Vision Pro is powered by Apple's M2 chip, known for its high performance and efficiency. This chip handles the complex processing required for rendering high-resolution graphics, managing sensor data, and running AR applications smoothly.

In addition to the M2, the device includes a dedicated R1 co-processor that specifically manages the real-time processing of data from the device's sensors. This ensures that the AR experience remains fluid and responsive, with minimal latency.

Apple Vision Pro runs on a new operating system called visionOS, which is optimized for AR and mixed reality experiences. The interface is designed to be intuitive and user-friendly, allowing users to navigate through apps, settings, and content with ease. Vision Pro introduces the concept of spatial computing, where digital elements are not confined to screens but exist and interact within the user's physical space. For example, users can place a virtual monitor on their desk or project a movie onto their living room wall. The device also incorporates haptic feedback, providing tactile sensations that enhance the sense of realism when interacting with virtual objects.

Applications and Use Cases

Vision Pro is positioned as a powerful tool for productivity, offering virtual desktops, immersive video conferencing, and the ability to interact with multiple apps simultaneously in a 3D space. Professionals can use the device to create expansive, customizable workspaces that go beyond the limitations of physical screens.

The device offers a new way to experience movies, games, and other media, with immersive visuals and spatial audio that make content feel more engaging and lifelike. Users can watch movies on a virtual screen that feels as large as a theater screen or play games that interact with their physical environment.

Vision Pro is also being adopted in educational and training contexts, where it can be used to create interactive simulations, virtual classrooms, and other learning experiences that leverage AR to make content more engaging and effective.

Apple has introduced several health-focused applications for Vision Pro, including virtual fitness trainers, meditation guides, and wellness tracking features. These apps utilize the immersive nature of the device to create more effective and personalized health experiences.

The **Apple Vision Pro** represents a significant milestone in the evolution of AR and mixed reality technologies. With its cutting-edge hardware, intuitive user interface, and wide range of applications, it has the potential to transform how we interact with the digital world. Whether for productivity, entertainment, education, or health, the Vision Pro is poised to be a central device in the future of computing.

SAMSUNG GALAXY Z FOLD 5

https://www.samsung.com/us/smartphones/galaxy-z-fold5/

The **Samsung Galaxy Z Fold 5**, released in 2023, represents the latest iteration in Samsung's pioneering foldable smartphone lineup. Building on the successes and lessons of its predecessors, the Z Fold 5 brings refined design, enhanced durability, and improved functionality, solidifying Samsung's leadership in the foldable smartphone market. Here's an in-depth look at what makes the Galaxy Z Fold 5 a standout device in 2023:

Design and Build

The Galaxy Z Fold 5 features a sleek and polished design, further refining the foldable form factor that Samsung introduced years ago. The device opens like a book, revealing a large inner display while maintaining a conventional smartphone screen on the outside when folded. The design continues to merge the best of both smartphones and tablets into one versatile device.

One of the most significant improvements in the Z Fold 5 is the new Flex Hinge, which allows the phone to close completely flat without any gap between the two halves. This hinge is more durable and slimmer than previous versions, contributing to a more refined and premium feel while also improving the phone's overall durability.

The Z Fold 5 is constructed with Samsung's Armor Aluminum frame and Gorilla Glass Victus 2, making it more resistant to

"

drops and scratches. The device also features an IPX8 water resistance rating, meaning it can withstand immersion in water up to 1.5 meters deep for up to 30 minutes, providing peace of mind against accidental spills and rain.

Display

The Galaxy Z Fold 5 boasts a 7.6-inch Dynamic AMOLED 2X main display with a 120Hz adaptive refresh rate. This large, vibrant screen is perfect for multitasking, gaming, and media consumption, offering an expansive canvas that adjusts dynamically to the content displayed.

When folded, the device offers a 6.2-inch Super AMOLED cover display with a 120Hz refresh rate. This outer screen is fully functional, allowing users to handle most smartphone tasks without opening the device, which adds to the convenience and practicality of the foldable design.

Both displays feature enhanced brightness levels, making them more readable in direct sunlight and improving the viewing experience in various lighting conditions.

Performance

The Galaxy Z Fold 5 is powered by a custom-tuned Snapdragon 8 Gen 2 for Galaxy chipset, which provides top-tier performance, optimized specifically for Samsung's flagship devices. This chipset ensures smooth multitasking, high-end gaming, and efficient power management.

The device comes with 12GB of RAM, ensuring smooth performance across apps and when multitasking. Storage options include 256GB, 512GB, and 1TB, catering to users with varying needs for space.

Despite its slim design, the Z Fold 5 is equipped with a 4,400mAh battery, offering solid battery life for a full day of use. The phone supports 25W fast charging, wireless charging, and reverse wireless charging, making it convenient for powering up on the go.

Software and Multitasking

The Galaxy Z Fold 5 runs Samsung's One UI 5.1.1, based on Android 13. This interface is optimized for foldable devices, offering enhanced multitasking features such as multi-window support, drag-and-drop functionality, and an improved taskbar that makes switching between apps more intuitive.

Flex Mode is a key feature of the Z Fold 5, allowing the device to stay open at various angles. This mode splits the screen into two functional areas, making it ideal for tasks like video calls, watching videos while taking notes, or using the device as a mini laptop.

The Z Fold 5 continues to support the S Pen, which is sold separately. This stylus transforms the device into a powerful tool for note-taking, drawing, and precision input, further enhancing productivity and creative capabilities.

Camera System

The Galaxy Z Fold 5 features a versatile triple-camera system on the back:

Primary Sensor: A 50MP wide-angle camera with optical image stabilization (OIS) that delivers sharp, high-quality photos and videos, even in low-light conditions.
Ultra-Wide Sensor: A 12MP ultra-wide camera that captures expansive shots with a 123-degree field of view, perfect for landscapes and group photos.
Telephoto Sensor: A 10MP telephoto camera with 3x optical zoom and OIS, allowing users to capture detailed shots from a distance.

The cover display houses a 10MP front camera for selfies and video calls, while the main inner display has a 4MP under-display camera, which is less noticeable than traditional punch-hole cameras and preserves the immersive experience of the large screen. Samsung's camera software on the Z Fold 5 includes a variety of shooting modes, AI enhancements, and Pro controls, offering flexibility and control for both casual photographers and enthusiasts. The device supports 8K video recording and advanced image stabilization for smooth, professional-looking videos.

Unique Features

The Z Fold 5's taskbar is customizable, allowing users to pin their favorite apps and access them quickly. This feature makes it easier to switch between apps, enhancing the multitasking experience.

The phone seamlessly transitions apps between the cover and main displays. Whether you're using an app on the cover screen and decide to unfold the device, the app expands smoothly to the larger screen without interruption.

With its powerful hardware, 120Hz displays, and large screen, the Z Fold 5 is particularly well-suited for gaming. Samsung has worked with game developers to optimize titles for the foldable display, ensuring a superior gaming experience.

The Samsung Galaxy Z Fold 5 represents the pinnacle of foldable smartphone technology in 2023. With its refined design, powerful performance, and enhanced multitasking capabilities, it appeals to users looking for a premium, versatile device that bridges the gap between smartphones and tablets. As foldable technology continues to evolve, the Z Fold 5 stands out as a testament to Samsung's innovation and commitment to pushing the boundaries of mobile technology.

NOTHING PHONE (2)

https://us.nothing.tech/pages/phone-2

The **Nothing Phone (2)**, released in 2023, is the second smartphone from the London-based tech company Nothing, founded by Carl Pei, co-founder of OnePlus. Building on the success and distinctive design of the original Nothing Phone (1), the Phone (2) aimed to further disrupt the smartphone market with its unique aesthetics, innovative features, and a strong focus on user experience. Here's a detailed look at what makes the Nothing Phone (2) stand out:

Design and Build

The most notable feature of the Nothing Phone (2) is its Glyph Interface, an evolution of the LED notification system introduced with the Phone (1). The back of the phone is made of transparent glass, revealing a set of customizable LED strips arranged in a unique pattern. These LEDs light up for various notifications, such as incoming calls, messages, charging status, and app alerts. Users can customize the lighting patterns and even set specific light combinations for different contacts or apps.

The Phone (2) continues with Nothing's minimalist design philosophy, featuring clean lines, a symmetrical frame, and a distinctive transparent back. The transparency showcases the phone's internal components, giving it a futuristic, industrial look. The phone comes in two color options: white and black, each emphasizing the LED Glyphs differently.

The device is constructed with high-quality materials, including an aluminum frame and Gorilla Glass on both the front and back, ensuring durability and a premium feel. It also has an IP54 rating, offering splash and dust resistance.

Display

The Nothing Phone (2) boasts a 6.7-inch OLED display with Full HD+ resolution. The screen delivers vibrant colors, deep blacks, and excellent contrast, making it ideal for media consumption and gaming.

The display features a 120Hz adaptive refresh rate, providing smooth scrolling and responsive touch interactions. This high refresh rate enhances the overall user experience, especially in gaming and navigating through the interface. The phone also includes an under-display fingerprint scanner, which offers quick and secure biometric authentication.

Performance

The Nothing Phone (2) is powered by the Qualcomm Snapdragon 8+ Gen 1 chipset, a significant upgrade over the mid-range processor in the Phone (1). This high-end processor delivers excellent performance for multitasking, gaming, and running demanding applications.

The phone comes in multiple configurations, with options for 8GB or 12GB of RAM and 128GB, 256GB, or 512GB of internal storage. This ensures that users have ample space for apps, media, and files, along with smooth multitasking capabilities.

The Phone (2) is equipped with a 4,700mAh battery, offering all-day battery life under typical usage conditions. It supports fast charging (up to 45W) and wireless charging (up to 15W), making it convenient to keep the device powered throughout the day.

Software and User Interface

The Nothing Phone (2) runs on Nothing OS 2.0, which is based on Android 13. The operating system is designed to be clean, minimal, and free of bloatware, staying true to Nothing's ethos of simplicity and efficiency. The UI features custom widgets, unique app icons, and a focus on usability.

Nothing OS 2.0 offers a high degree of customization, allowing users to personalize the home screen, notification settings, and even the Glyph Interface. The minimalist UI is designed to reduce distractions and provide a streamlined user experience.

Camera System

The Nothing Phone (2) features a dual-camera system on the rear, consisting of a 50MP primary sensor and a 50MP ultra-wide sensor. The cameras are designed to deliver high-quality images with excellent detail, dynamic range, and color accuracy.

Primary Sensor: The primary camera is a 50MP Sony IMX890 sensor with optical image stabilization (OIS). It excels in various lighting conditions, offering sharp and vibrant photos. The OIS helps reduce blur in low-light scenarios and during handheld photography.

Ultra-Wide Sensor: The 50MP ultra-wide camera captures expansive shots with minimal distortion, making it ideal for landscape photography and group photos.

The front-facing camera is a 32MP sensor, housed in a punch-hole cutout on the display. It offers clear and detailed selfies, with support for portrait mode and AI enhancements. The camera app on the Nothing Phone (2) includes various shooting modes, such as Night Mode, Portrait Mode, and Pro Mode, allowing users to adjust settings manually for more creative control. The phone also supports 4K video recording at 60fps.

Innovative Features

A new feature introduced with the Phone (2) is the Glyph Composer, which allows users to create their own custom ringtones and notification sounds using the LED Glyphs. This feature enhances personalization, letting users match sound and light patterns to their preferences.

The Phone (2) supports reverse wireless charging, enabling users to charge other devices, such as earbuds or smartwatches, by placing them on the back of the phone.

Nothing has emphasized sustainability in the design and production of the Phone (2). The device is made with recycled materials, and the packaging is plastic-free. The company also commits to long-term software support, ensuring the phone remains usable for several years.

The Nothing Phone (2) is a bold and innovative device that builds on the foundation laid by its predecessor. With its unique Glyph Interface, high-performance specs, and focus on user experience, it offers a compelling alternative to traditional smartphones. Whether for its customizable lighting system, minimalist design, or advanced features, the Phone (2) has made a significant impact in 2023, demonstrating that there's still room for innovation and creativity in the smartphone market.

TESLA CYBERTRUCK

https://www.tesla.com/cybertruck

The **Tesla Cybertruck** is one of the most anticipated electric vehicles (EVs) of the decade. First unveiled in 2019 by Elon Musk, the Cybertruck has captured the public's imagination with its futuristic design, cutting-edge technology, and bold promises of performance and durability. After years of anticipation, 2023 marked the beginning of its production, with deliveries finally commencing toward the end of the year. The Cybertruck's pricing has seen an increase from its initial announcement, with the base model now starting at around $60,990, going up to $99,990 for the top-tier model. Tesla has positioned the Cybertruck as a key player in the transition to sustainable energy, aiming to challenge traditional fossil-fuel-powered trucks on the market. Here's a detailed overview of what makes the Tesla Cybertruck a unique and groundbreaking vehicle:

Design and Build

The Tesla Cybertruck is unlike any other vehicle on the road. Its design is highly angular and minimalist, featuring sharp lines and flat surfaces that give it a distinctly futuristic, almost science fiction-like appearance. The exterior is reminiscent of something out of a dystopian movie, making it a standout in the automotive world.

The Cybertruck's body is constructed from ultra-hard 30X cold-rolled stainless steel, which Tesla refers to as an "exoskeleton." This material is designed to be incredibly durable, resistant to dents, damage, and corrosion. Tesla has demonstrated the vehicle's toughness by showing it can withstand impacts that would severely damage other cars.

The Cybertruck is equipped with Tesla Armor Glass, a special type of reinforced glass that is designed to be more resistant to shattering. Although there were some publicized issues during its initial unveiling, Tesla has since worked on improving the glass's durability.

The Cybertruck is large and imposing, with dimensions comparable to or larger than traditional full-size pickup trucks. Its size and design prioritize utility, with a spacious bed and a strong, commanding presence on the road.

Performance

The Cybertruck has powertrain options available in multiple configurations, each offering different levels of performance:

The base model features a single motor and rear-wheel drive, offering a good balance of performance and range. The Dual Motor All-Wheel Drive (AWD) configuration adds a second motor, providing better traction and significantly improved acceleration and towing capacity. The top-tier version features three motors, delivering extreme performance with lightning-fast acceleration, superior off-road capability, and the highest towing capacity.

The Tri-Motor version of the Cybertruck is particularly notable for its speed, with a 0-60 mph time of under 2.9 seconds, making it one of the fastest trucks ever produced. The Cybertruck offers an impressive range across its various models, with the highest configuration expected to achieve over 500 miles on a single charge, thanks to Tesla's advanced battery technology. And don't forget about towing and payload capacity. The Cybertruck is designed for heavy-duty use, with a maximum towing capacity of up to 14,000 pounds in the Tri-Motor configuration, and a payload capacity of up to 3,500 pounds. These numbers make it a strong contender against traditional internal combustion engine (ICE) trucks.

Interior and Features

Inside, the Cybertruck continues Tesla's minimalist design philosophy. The dashboard is simple and clean, dominated by a large 17-inch touchscreen display that controls most of the vehicle's functions. The interior materials are durable and functional, in line with the truck's rugged design. The Cybertruck offers seating for up to six people, with ample legroom and headroom. The seats are designed for comfort during long drives, and the rear seats can fold down to increase storage space.

As expected from Tesla, the Cybertruck is loaded with technology. The vehicle comes equipped with Tesla's Autopilot system, offering advanced driver-assistance features like lane-keeping, adaptive cruise control, and automatic emergency braking. Full Self-Driving (FSD) capability is available as an option, allowing for autonomous driving in the future as software updates are released.

The Cybertruck features a large, 6.5-foot bed, which Tesla refers to as the "vault." The bed is enclosed with a retractable, roll-up cover that enhances security and aerodynamics. It also has built-in power outlets, a compressed air compressor, and the capability to carry up to 3,500 pounds of cargo, making it extremely versatile for work and recreational use. The Cybertruck comes with an adaptive air suspension system that allows the vehicle's ride height to be adjusted for different driving conditions. This feature is particularly useful for off-roading, where the suspension can be raised to increase ground clearance.

Off-Road Capabilities

The Cybertruck is designed to handle tough terrains, thanks to its high ground clearance, powerful motors, and robust construction. Its approach and departure angles are competitive with traditional off-road vehicles, making it suitable for a variety of outdoor adventures. The dual and tri-motor versions of the Cybertruck come with an advanced all-wheel-drive system, providing excellent traction on challenging surfaces such as mud, snow, and sand.

Sustainability

As an all-electric vehicle, the Cybertruck produces zero tailpipe emissions, contributing to a reduction in greenhouse gasses and air pollution. This aligns with Tesla's mission to accelerate the world's transition to sustainable energy. Tesla has also emphasized the use of sustainable materials in the construction of the Cybertruck, including recycled stainless steel for the exoskeleton.

The Tesla Cybertruck is more than just a vehicle; it's a bold statement about the future of transportation. With its distinctive design, advanced technology, and high-performance capabilities, the Cybertruck is set to redefine what people expect from trucks and electric vehicles in general. While it's not for everyone, its impact on the automotive industry is undeniable, and it will likely remain a significant topic of conversation and influence for years to come.

DJI MAVIC 3 PRO

https://www.dji.com/mavic-3-pro

The **DJI Mavic 3 Pro**, released in 2023, is a top-tier drone that represents the pinnacle of DJI's innovation in aerial photography and videography. As the successor to the Mavic 2 Pro, the Mavic 3 Pro brings significant upgrades in camera technology, flight performance, and smart features, making it one of the most advanced consumer drones on the market. Here's an in-depth look at what makes the DJI Mavic 3 Pro stand out:

Design and Build

Like its predecessors, the Mavic 3 Pro features a foldable design that makes it highly portable. Despite its advanced capabilities, the drone remains compact and lightweight, making it easy to transport and deploy in various locations. DJI has refined the design of the Mavic 3 Pro to improve aerodynamics, resulting in more efficient flight and better stability in various weather conditions. The drone's sleek body reduces drag, contributing to longer flight times and smoother flight performance.

Camera System

One of the most significant upgrades in the Mavic 3 Pro is its triple-camera system, a first for DJI drones. This array includes:

20MP 4/3 CMOS Hasselblad camera, which offers incredible image quality, dynamic range, and color accuracy. The larger sensor size allows for better low-light performance and more detailed photos and videos.

12MP camera with a 7x optical zoom and a 28x hybrid zoom, enabling users to capture distant subjects with clarity. This camera is particularly useful for wildlife photography, surveillance, and any scenario where getting closer to the subject is not feasible.

48MP ultra-wide-angle camera with a 108° field of view. This camera is ideal for capturing expansive landscapes and dramatic wide shots, adding versatility to the Mavic 3 Pro's shooting capabilities.

The Mavic 3 Pro excels in videography, supporting 5.1K video recording at 50fps and 4K at up to 120fps. This allows for ultra-high-definition footage and slow-motion video, catering to professional filmmakers and content creators.

DJI's collaboration with Hasselblad brings the HNCS technology to the Mavic 3 Pro, ensuring that colors are rendered naturally and accurately without the need for extensive post-processing. This feature is particularly beneficial for photographers who demand high color fidelity in their work.

The Mavic 3 Pro supports 10-bit D-Log and HLG color profiles, offering greater flexibility in color grading during post-production. This capability is crucial for professional videographers who need to match footage from different cameras or apply complex color effects.

Flight Performance

The Mavic 3 Pro boasts an impressive flight time of up to 46 minutes on a single charge, one of the longest in its class. This extended flight time allows for longer sessions in the air without frequent interruptions for battery changes.

DJI's O3+ transmission system provides a reliable and strong connection between the drone and the remote controller, offering a range of up to 15 kilometers (9.3 miles) in optimal conditions. This system ensures stable video transmission at 1080p/60fps, allowing pilots to see exactly what the drone's camera is capturing in real-time.

The Mavic 3 Pro has enhanced motors and propellers that provide better stability and wind resistance. This allows the drone to maintain steady flight in more challenging weather conditions, making it suitable for a wider range of environments.

Smart Features and Autonomy

The Mavic 3 Pro features an omnidirectional obstacle sensing system with multiple vision sensors placed around the drone. This system provides comprehensive awareness of the drone's surroundings, enabling advanced obstacle avoidance and smoother flight paths, even in complex environments.

DJI's latest iteration of its tracking technology, ActiveTrack 5.0, is included in the Mavic 3 Pro. This feature allows the drone to follow a subject automatically, keeping it in the frame while avoiding obstacles. The improved algorithms offer more precise tracking, even when the subject moves unpredictably.

MasterShots is an intelligent mode that allows users to capture cinematic sequences with minimal effort. By selecting a subject, the drone will automatically perform a series of predefined maneuvers and capture the footage, which can then be easily edited into a polished video.

The Waypoint 3.0 feature enables users to create complex flight paths with pre-programmed points of interest. This feature is particularly useful for capturing time-lapses, survey missions, or any scenario where consistent flight patterns are required.

QuickShots are pre-programmed flight maneuvers that capture

short, dynamic video clips. These include Dronie, Circle, Helix, Rocket, Boomerang, and Asteroid, allowing users to create visually engaging content with minimal manual input.

Software and Compatibility

The Mavic 3 Pro is compatible with the DJI Fly app, which provides an intuitive interface for controlling the drone, adjusting camera settings, and accessing smart features. The app also offers tutorials and tips for beginners, making it easier to learn how to operate the drone effectively.

The Mavic 3 Pro integrates seamlessly with other DJI products and services, such as the DJI RC Pro remote controller, DJI Goggles for immersive FPV flying, and DJI's cloud services for data storage and sharing.

DJI offers powerful post-processing tools like DJI Terra for mapping and photogrammetry, and DJI's own editing software, allowing users to get the most out of the high-quality footage captured by the Mavic 3 Pro.

Safety and Compliance

The Mavic 3 Pro is equipped with geofencing technology that helps prevent the drone from entering restricted airspace. DJI's software provides real-time updates on no-fly zones, ensuring that users operate their drones safely and within legal boundaries.

The Mavic 3 Pro includes an enhanced RTH feature that automatically returns the drone to its takeoff point if the battery is low or if it loses connection with the controller. The drone uses its obstacle avoidance sensors to find the safest path back, reducing the risk of accidents during the return flight.

Use Cases

The Mavic 3 Pro is an excellent tool for filmmakers who require high-quality aerial footage. Its advanced camera system, along with support for 10-bit color and 5.1K resolution, makes it suitable for producing content that can be used in commercials, documentaries, and feature films.

For professional photographers, the Mavic 3 Pro offers unprecedented flexibility in capturing still images from the air. The combination of a large sensor, Hasselblad color science, and versatile zoom capabilities allows photographers to capture images that would be impossible from the ground.

Beyond photography and videography, the Mavic 3 Pro is also used in industrial applications such as surveying, mapping, and inspections. Its precise flight controls, long-range transmission, and high-resolution cameras make it a valuable tool for professionals in these fields.

The DJI Mavic 3 Pro is a masterpiece of drone technology, offering unparalleled camera capabilities, flight performance, and smart features. It is designed to meet the needs of professionals who demand the highest quality in their aerial work, as well as enthusiasts who want to explore the full potential of drone photography and videography. With its advanced technology and robust design, the Mavic 3 Pro is set to remain a leader in the drone market for years to come.

AMAZON ASTRO

https://www.amazon.com/Astro

The Amazon Astro is a home robot designed to assist with various household tasks, such as security monitoring, delivering items around the house, and providing reminders. With its AI-powered capabilities, cute design, and integration with Alexa, Astro represented a significant step forward in the development of personal robots for everyday use.

Design and Features

Astro is a robot with a screen for a face that can express emotions and interact with users. It's equipped with wheels to move around your home and has a compact design to navigate through tight spaces.

It uses advanced navigation and intelligent motion technology to autonomously move around the house, avoiding obstacles and reaching specific locations as needed. Astro is equipped with cameras, including a periscope camera that can extend to give it a higher view of the surroundings. It integrates with Amazon's Ring security ecosystem, allowing it to patrol your home, detect unusual activities, and alert you via your phone.

Astro is deeply integrated with Amazon's Alexa, meaning it can do everything an Alexa device can, such as controlling smart home devices, answering questions, playing music, and more.

You can use Astro to make video calls, watch videos, or listen to music. The robot can follow you around the house, ensuring you don't miss a moment.

Astro can carry small items, deliver them to specific people in the house, and even monitor specific rooms for activity or disturbances. It can also remind you of tasks or routines.

Amazon has included privacy features like "Do Not Disturb" mode, where Astro will remain stationary and inactive until reactivated. There's also a physical button to disable the cameras and microphones.

Use Cases

Astro can help monitor elderly family members, ensuring their safety and even alerting caregivers if something seems wrong. Astro can be used to patrol the home, check for any security breaches, and provide real-time video feed to your phone. If you're away from home, Astro can be used to check in on your pets, monitor your house, and ensure everything is in order.

Concerns

Given the extensive monitoring and the integration with Amazon's services, there are concerns about privacy and the extent of data collection.

Astro is relatively expensive, with a price tag that may be prohibitive for some consumers. It was initially available by invitation only, and the price was around $999.99 during the early access phase.

While Astro has many capabilities, some critics argue that it may be more of a novelty than a necessity, especially in households that already have several smart devices.

Amazon Astro represents a significant step in consumer

robotics, offering a blend of home security, smart home integration, and entertainment. While it's a promising device, it may still be a few iterations away from becoming a household staple, given the concerns and current limitations.

PELOTON GUIDE

https://www.onepeloton.com/guide

The Peloton Guide is a strength training device that expands Peloton's offerings beyond its well-known cycling and treadmill equipment. Released in 2022, the Peloton Guide is designed to bring interactive and personalized strength training into the home. Here's an overview of its features, functionalities, and what sets it apart:

Design and Setup

The Peloton Guide is a compact, camera-like device that connects to your TV. It comes with a simple remote and can be set up easily on top of or next to your TV. It connects to your TV via HDMI and to your Wi-Fi network. Once connected, it integrates with the Peloton app and other Peloton equipment you may have.

Key Features

One of the standout features of the Peloton Guide is its AI-powered body tracking technology. The device uses its camera to track your movements and form during workouts. This feature helps ensure that you're performing exercises correctly and safely, reducing the risk of injury.

This feature encourages users to complete their workout by tracking their movements throughout each exercise. The Guide can identify whether you're actively participating in the workout or slacking, and it will remind you to stay engaged.

The Peloton Guide can count your reps during specific exercises, giving you real-time feedback on your performance. It can also integrate with heart rate monitors to give you more detailed insights into your workout intensity.

Peloton Guide users have access to Peloton's extensive library of strength training classes. The classes are led by professional instructors and vary in difficulty, duration, and focus area (e.g., upper body, lower body, full body).

Based on your performance and activity, the Peloton Guide provides personalized class recommendations. Over time, it learns your preferences and fitness level, suggesting workouts that are best suited for you. You can use the Peloton app to track your progress, schedule workouts, and explore new classes. The app also provides detailed analytics on your performance.

The device supports voice commands, allowing you to start or stop workouts, navigate menus, and control the volume without needing to use the remote.

Strength Training Focus

Unlike Peloton's bike and treadmill, which focus primarily on cardio, the Peloton Guide is all about strength training. The classes involve a variety of exercises such as weight lifting, bodyweight exercises, and resistance training.

The device provides guidance on form and technique, ensuring you get the most out of your strength training sessions. It's like having a personal trainer at home, helping you improve your form and efficiency.

Price and Subscription

The Peloton Guide was initially priced at around $295, making it one of the more affordable entry points into the Peloton ecosystem.

A Peloton All-Access Membership is required to use the Guide, which costs $44 per month. This membership provides access to the full range of Peloton classes, including those for cycling, running, yoga, meditation, and strength training.

The Peloton Guide is a unique addition to the home fitness market, offering AI-driven insights and guidance for strength training. It caters to both beginners and experienced users, providing personalized workout experiences that can help improve technique and results. For those already invested in the Peloton ecosystem or looking to start strength training at home, the Peloton Guide offers a compelling option with its interactive and immersive approach.

WITHINGS U-SCAN

https://www.withings.com/us/en/u-scan

The Withings U-Scan is an innovative health monitoring device designed to analyze urine from the comfort of your home. Launched by Withings, a company known for its health-focused smart devices, the U-Scan provides users with detailed insights into their health by analyzing biomarkers in their urine. Here's an overview of its features, functionality, and potential impact on personal health management:

Design and Setup

The Withings U-Scan is a small, circular device designed to fit inside your toilet bowl. It's sleek and discreet, blending seamlessly into the bathroom environment. The device is easy to install; it attaches to the side of the toilet bowl. It is designed to withstand the environment of the toilet and remain secure while in use.

Key Features

The primary function of the U-Scan is to analyze urine for a variety of biomarkers. Urine is a rich source of information about the body, containing data on hydration, nutrient levels, and metabolic functions.

The U-Scan uses interchangeable cartridges, each designed to analyze specific biomarkers. Different cartridges can be used for different purposes, such as monitoring hydration, nutrition, hormone levels, or detecting specific health conditions. The device allows for daily testing, providing regular feedback on health metrics. This can help users track changes in their health over time and adjust their lifestyle or diet accordingly.

The data collected by U-Scan is synced with the Withings Health Mate app, where users can view detailed reports and trends. The app provides insights and recommendations based on the analysis, helping users make informed decisions about their health. The U-Scan can differentiate between users based on their unique urine stream signature, ensuring that the data is personalized for each household member.

Health Monitoring Applications

The U-Scan can monitor hydration levels by analyzing specific gravity and other urine characteristics, helping users stay properly hydrated. It can assess the balance of nutrients, such as vitamin C or ketones, providing insights into dietary needs and effectiveness of diets like keto.

For women, U-Scan can track hormone levels related to menstrual cycles, providing information on fertility windows or potential hormonal imbalances.

In the future, Withings plans to expand the U-Scan's capabilities to detect early signs of various diseases, including chronic conditions like diabetes or kidney disease.

Privacy and Data Security

Withings emphasizes privacy, ensuring that all data is encrypted and securely stored. Users have control over who can access their health information through the app. The U-Scan processes the initial data locally, with more complex analysis conducted in the cloud, where advanced algorithms can provide detailed insights.

Usage and Maintenance

Cartridges need to be replaced periodically, depending on the type of analysis being performed. Withings plans to offer various cartridges for different health monitoring needs. The device is designed to have a long battery life, minimizing the need for frequent recharges.

Cost and Availability

The U-Scan is a premium health device, with the initial cost expected to be in the higher range for consumer health gadgets. The price includes the device and a starting set of cartridges. **Withings** may offer a subscription service for the ongoing delivery of cartridges, similar to how other health monitoring devices operate.

The Withings U-Scan represents a significant advancement in personal health monitoring, bringing lab-grade urine analysis into the home. It offers a convenient and non-invasive way to track important health metrics daily, empowering users to take proactive control over their health. While it's particularly useful for hydration and nutritional monitoring, its potential for early disease detection and hormone tracking could make it a valuable tool for a wide range of users. As with all health devices, the effectiveness and accuracy will be key to its long-term success, and it will be interesting to see how it integrates into broader health management practices.

ANKER 757 POWERHOUSE

https://www.anker.com/products/a1770111?ref=the-complete-guide-to-understanding-anker-757-powerhouse

The Anker 757 PowerHouse is a high-capacity portable power station designed for those who need reliable power in various situations, whether for outdoor adventures, emergency backup, or off-grid living. Here's a detailed overview of its features, functionalities, and potential use cases:

Design and Build

The Anker 757 PowerHouse has a rugged, industrial design with a sturdy build to withstand rough handling. It features a handle for easy transport and a durable exterior to protect against impacts and the elements.

It is relatively compact for its power capacity but still substantial, weighing around 48 pounds (22 kg). Its size and weight make it less portable compared to smaller power stations but manageable for car camping or emergency use.

Power Capacity and Output

The 757 PowerHouse boasts a large battery capacity of 1,229Wh (watt-hours), providing substantial power for extended use. This capacity is suitable for running multiple devices or larger appliances for significant periods.

It offers a peak output of 1,500W (watts) and can handle

surge loads up to 3,000W. This makes it capable of powering high-wattage devices like refrigerators, power tools, or small appliances.

The PowerHouse is equipped with a variety of output ports, including:

Multiple AC outlets for standard home appliances. Several USB-A and USB-C ports for charging devices like smartphones, tablets, and laptops. It also has 12V car ports for powering vehicle accessories or small electronics.

Charging and Recharging

The PowerHouse supports solar charging, allowing you to recharge it using compatible solar panels. This is especially useful for off-grid scenarios or extended outdoor trips. The charging speed will depend on the wattage of the solar panels used.

It can be recharged via a standard AC outlet, making it versatile for home use. Charging times will vary based on the power source and current battery level. There is also the option to recharge the PowerHouse using a 12V car charger, which is convenient for recharging on the go.

Features and Functionality

The PowerHouse includes an LCD screen that displays critical information such as battery level, power consumption, and input/output status. This helps users monitor and manage power usage effectively.

It incorporates intelligent battery management systems to ensure safe and efficient charging and discharging. This includes protection against overcharging, overheating, and short circuits. The PowerHouse is designed to maximize energy efficiency, providing high performance with minimal energy loss.

Use Cases

Ideal for camping, RVing, or tailgating, where reliable power is needed for lighting, cooking, or powering gadgets. It can serve as a backup power source during power outages, supporting essential devices like medical equipment, refrigerators, or communication tools. The PowerHouse is very useful for remote locations where traditional power sources are unavailable, providing a dependable power supply for everyday needs.

Price and Availability

The Anker 757 PowerHouse is positioned in the higher end of the portable power station market, with pricing reflecting its large capacity and high power output. The exact price may vary based on the retailer and any promotions. It is available through various online retailers, including Anker's official website, Amazon, and other electronics stores.

The Anker 757 PowerHouse is a powerful and versatile portable power station, designed for users who need substantial power capacity and flexibility. With its high capacity, multiple output options, and support for solar and car charging, it's a robust solution for outdoor activities, emergency situations, and off-grid living. Its rugged design and smart features make it a reliable choice for those seeking a high-performance power source in various scenarios.

SONY WH-1000XM5

https://electronics.sony.com/audio/headphones/
headband/p/wh1000xm5-b

The Sony WH-1000XM5 headphones, released in 2023, continue to define excellence in noise-canceling and audio performance. Here's an overview of their key features and specifications:
Key Features:

The WH-1000XM5 uses advanced noise-canceling technology, powered by two processors controlling multiple microphones. This setup allows for unprecedented noise reduction, effectively blocking out ambient noise from environments such as airplanes and busy streets.

Enhanced by Sony's V1 processor, the headphones deliver superior sound quality. The integration of DSEE Extreme technology upscales compressed digital music files in real time, bringing you closer to the quality of high-resolution audio.

The WH-1000XM5 features a sleek, minimalist design with a lightweight construction, making them comfortable for extended listening sessions. The ear cups have been ergonomically redesigned for a better fit and enhanced sound isolation.

These headphones offer up to 30 hours of battery life with noise canceling on, ensuring long-lasting performance during travel or extended use. Additionally, a quick charging feature gives you up to 3 hours of playtime from just a 3-minute charge.

Intuitive touch-sensor controls on the ear cups allow you to manage playback, calls, and activate voice assistants without needing to pull out your phone.

With Precise Voice Pickup technology, the WH-1000XM5 improves call quality by precisely controlling the five microphones built into the headphones and performing advanced audio signal processing.

Automatic pause and play are available through a feature that detects whether you are wearing the headphones. They also offer Adaptive Sound Control, which senses your activity and location, adjusting ambient sound settings accordingly for the ideal listening experience.

The headphones support Bluetooth 5.2 connectivity, ensuring a stable and quick pairing process with a wide range of devices. They also support LDAC codec for high-resolution audio listening over Bluetooth.

The Sony WH-1000XM5 is priced competitively and targets audiophiles and regular commuters looking for top-tier audio performance with industry-leading noise cancellation.

FITBIT SENSE 2

https://www.fitbit.com/global/us/products/
smartwatches/sense2

The Fitbit Sense 2, launched in 2023, is a top-tier health and fitness smartwatch designed to provide comprehensive wellness tracking. Here's an overview of its features and functionality:

Key Features:

The Sense 2 offers extensive health monitoring capabilities, including an ECG app, stress management, sleep tracking with a Sleep Profile feature, and a Daily Readiness Score that advises on workout intensity based on recovery, sleep, and heart rate variability.

The device includes a new continuous electrodermal activity (cEDA) sensor to monitor stress levels, a high-precision heart rate monitor, and sensors for skin temperature variation and SpO2 levels.

Alongside health features, the Sense 2 supports notifications for calls, texts, and smartphone apps. It also includes built-in GPS, Google Wallet, and Google Maps, enhancing its utility as a daily smartwatch.

The Fitbit Sense 2 maintains a long battery life, offering over 6 days on a single charge, ensuring users can track their health and activities without frequent recharges.

It sports a sleek and modern design with a vibrant display that is easy to navigate and customize with various watch faces and always-on display settings.

Fitbit offers a 6-month trial of Fitbit Premium with the purchase of a Sense 2. This service provides deeper analytics, personalized insights, and guided health and fitness programs.

The Fitbit Sense 2 is priced at $299.95. It's available in several color options and can be purchased directly from Fitbit's official website or through major retailers.

APPLE WATCH SERIES 9

https://www.apple.com/apple-watch-series-9

The Apple Watch Series 9, released in 2023, enhances its functionality with new features and powerful performance upgrades, setting a new standard for smartwatches. Here's a breakdown of the key features and improvements:

Key Features and Innovations:

The Series 9 is equipped with Apple's custom silicon, featuring a dual-core CPU with 5.6 billion transistors—60% more than the previous S8 chip. This increase in processing power allows for faster and more efficient performance. The four-core Neural Engine processes machine learning tasks up to twice as fast as before, enhancing the overall user experience.

The watch is available in 41mm and 45mm sizes and comes in various finishes including starlight, midnight, silver, (PRODUCT)RED, and a new pink aluminum case. Stainless steel options are available in gold, silver, and graphite. The design is both modern and functional, built to withstand the rigors of daily wear.

It continues to offer a Retina display with Force Touch technology, ensuring vivid colors and easy navigation through a touch interface.

The Series 9 maintains its focus on health with features like an ECG app, blood oxygen monitoring, and an enhanced workout suite that tracks a wide range of activities from running to yoga.

Despite its enhanced capabilities, the Series 9 maintains a robust battery life, offering all-day endurance on a single charge, with fast charging capabilities to quickly get back to full power.

New software features include the introduction of the double-tap gesture, making interactions simpler and more intuitive. The watch runs on the latest version of watchOS, which brings new health and fitness features, more customizable watch faces, and improved integration with iOS devices.

The Apple Watch Series 9 starts at $399 for the aluminum version in the smaller 41mm size. The pricing varies based on the model and band selection.

RING ALWAYS HOME CAM

https://ring.com/always-home-cam-flying-camera

The Ring Always Home Cam is a novel indoor flying security camera designed by Ring, offering a unique approach to home surveillance. This autonomous drone can navigate your home on predefined flight paths, providing a 360-degree view of any room it's directed to. This feature is particularly useful for checking in on different parts of your home while you're away, directly through the Ring app.

Key Features:

The camera flies autonomously along predetermined paths set by the user, making it possible to monitor multiple areas of your home without installing numerous static cameras.

When linked with Ring Alarm, the camera automatically deploys if specific sensors are triggered, enhancing home security by providing immediate visual feedback of disturbances.

The Always Home Cam is designed with privacy in mind; it only records video when it is undocked and flying along its path. When docked, the camera is physically blocked.

It streams and records video at a resolution of 1440x1440 HD and has a built-in rechargeable battery. The device operates within temperatures from 32°F to 100°F (0°C to 40°C) and requires a dual-band WiFi connection for optimal functionality.

As of now, the Always Home Cam is available for purchase by invitation only, directly from Amazon.

These gadgets from 2023 represent significant advancements in their respective fields, showcasing the ongoing innovation and creativity in technology. From enhancing daily life with smarter, more connected devices to pushing the boundaries of what's possible in health, entertainment, and personal productivity, these gadgets have set the stage for even more exciting developments in the years to come.

AI & ROBOTICS

Here are some fun and intriguing facts about advancements in AI and robotics from 2023 that are making a significant impact on daily life:

AI-Powered Personal Assistants

AI personal assistants, like those in smartphones and smart speakers, have become remarkably sophisticated. They can now engage in more natural and context-aware conversations, understanding nuanced queries and providing tailored responses.

Robotics in Healthcare

Robotic-assisted surgeries have become more precise and less invasive. In 2023, robots are performing complex procedures with higher accuracy, reducing recovery times and improving patient outcomes. Social robots like those designed for elder care can now recognize and respond to emotional cues, offering companionship and support to the elderly, improving their quality of life.

Autonomous Vehicles

Self-driving cars are incorporating advanced AI algorithms to enhance safety. They can predict and respond to potential hazards more effectively, making autonomous driving safer and more reliable. Some cities are experimenting with autonomous buses and shuttles, providing convenient and efficient public transportation options without human drivers.

AI in Creativity

AI algorithms can now create impressive art, music, and even write poetry. These tools are assisting artists and musicians by providing inspiration or creating unique pieces on their own. AI can generate realistic text, images, and videos, leading to new forms of digital content and entertainment. This includes deepfakes, which have become more convincing but also raise ethical considerations.

Smart Home Innovations

Household robots are becoming more advanced. For example, robots that can clean, cook, or even fold laundry are becoming more capable and affordable, making daily chores easier. Smart home systems use AI to optimize energy usage, reducing costs and environmental impact by automatically adjusting heating, cooling, and lighting based on usage patterns and preferences.

Advanced AI in Education

AI-driven educational tools can tailor learning experiences to individual students' needs, helping them progress at their own pace and improving educational outcomes. AI-powered virtual tutors provide additional support to students outside the classroom, offering explanations and help with homework on demand.

AI in Environmental Protection

AI and robotics are used for monitoring wildlife and tracking animal populations. Drones and AI analysis help conservationists gather data and protect endangered species more effectively. AI is being employed to monitor air and water quality, providing real-time data on pollution levels and helping cities manage environmental issues more proactively.

AI in Finance

AI-driven financial advisors offer personalized investment advice and portfolio management, making financial planning more accessible and tailored to individual needs. AI algorithms are increasingly adept at detecting fraudulent activities in real-time, enhancing security in financial transactions and reducing the risk of fraud.

Enhanced Human-Robot Interaction

Robots are being developed with the ability to recognize and respond to human emotions, making interactions more intuitive and natural. In workplaces, collaborative robots (cobots) are working alongside humans, assisting with tasks, and increasing productivity in industries like manufacturing and logistics.

AI for Mental Health

AI-driven mental health apps and platforms provide support for managing stress, anxiety, and depression, offering tools for therapy and self-care. AI systems that can understand and respond to emotional states are being used to provide support and companionship, enhancing mental health care.

These advancements reflect how AI and robotics are increasingly integrated into everyday life, enhancing convenience, safety, and productivity while also opening up new possibilities for creativity and personal growth.

SPACE AND SCIENCE

In 2023, space exploration and scientific research saw several significant achievements and discoveries. Here are some of the highlights:

James Webb Space Telescope (JWST) Discoveries

https://science.nasa.gov/mission/webb/

JWST made headlines with its detailed observations of exoplanet atmospheres. It provided new insights into the composition and weather patterns of distant planets, including detecting signs of water vapor and other potential habitability markers. The telescope captured some of the most detailed images of the early universe yet, revealing the formation of galaxies and stellar structures shortly after the Big Bang.

Mars Missions

https://mars.nasa.gov/

NASA's Perseverance rover continued its exploration of Mars, conducting in-depth analysis of Martian rocks and soil. Key findings included evidence of ancient river channels and delta formations, which provide clues about Mars' past water activity. The Ingenuity Mars helicopter achieved several successful flights, surpassing expectations and providing valuable aerial views of the Martian surface, aiding in the planning of rover routes and scientific investigations.

Artemis I Mission

https://www.nasa.gov/specials/artemis-i/

NASA's Artemis I mission, an uncrewed test flight of the Space Launch System (SLS) rocket and Orion spacecraft, successfully completed its mission, marking a significant step towards returning humans to the Moon. It tested critical systems and paved the way for future crewed missions.

China's Lunar Exploration

http://www.cnsa.gov.cn/

China's Chang'e 6 mission successfully returned lunar samples to Earth. This mission provided new lunar material for analysis, helping scientists understand the Moon's geological history and evolution.

Commercial Space Travel

https://www.spacex.com/

SpaceX continued to make strides with its Falcon 9 and Falcon Heavy rockets. Notably, the company launched and recovered several successful missions, including crewed flights to the International Space Station (ISS) and satellite deployments. Blue Origin's New Shepard rocket conducted multiple suborbital flights, bringing private passengers closer to space tourism and expanding commercial spaceflight opportunities.

Asteroid Exploration

https://science.nasa.gov/osiris-rex
https://www.nasa.gov/

NASA's OSIRIS-REx spacecraft, which had previously collected samples from the asteroid Bennu, successfully returned its sample capsule to Earth. The analysis of these samples is expected to provide significant insights into the early solar system.

Space Science and Technology Innovations

https://www.nasa.gov/

Advances in reusable rocket technology continued to evolve, with both SpaceX and Blue Origin improving their systems to make space travel more cost-effective and sustainable. New satellite missions, including Earth observation satellites and communication satellites, were launched to improve climate monitoring, disaster response, and global connectivity.

Extraterrestrial Life Search

https://www.seti.org/

The Search for Extraterrestrial Intelligence (SETI) made progress with new observational techniques and data analysis methods, enhancing the search for signs of intelligent life beyond Earth.

International Collaboration

http://www.globalspaceexploration.org/

The International Space Station continued to be a hub for international collaboration, with various nations contributing to scientific research and technology development. This included experiments in microgravity and the advancement of space technologies.

Space Debris Management
https://sdup.esoc.esa.int/
https://orbitaldebris.jsc.nasa.gov/

Efforts to address space debris were bolstered with new technologies and international agreements aimed at reducing the risk of collisions and ensuring the long-term sustainability of space operations.

These highlights reflect the rapid advancements in space exploration and science, showcasing humanity's growing capabilities and curiosity about the cosmos. Each of these achievements contributes to our understanding of space and our place within it, pushing the boundaries of what is possible in space exploration and technology.

.

CHAPTER 3:

Pop Culture Highlights of 2023

Top Movies & TV Shows

Here's a roundup of trivia about the biggest blockbusters, streaming hits, and surprise indie successes from 2023:

BIGGEST BLOCKBUSTERS OF 2023

1. **"Barbie" - Director:** Greta Gerwig

"Barbie" became one of the highest-grossing films of 2023, achieving significant commercial success and contributing to its strong cultural footprint. The film received widespread critical acclaim for its screenplay, direction, and performances, with many critics praising its fresh take on a classic character.

The film featured vibrant, colorful set designs that paid homage to the classic Barbie doll aesthetics while also introducing modern, whimsical elements. The movie included references to various Barbie dolls from different eras, creating a nostalgic experience for fans of all ages.

Trivia: The film's marketing campaign was as colorful and playful as the movie itself, featuring life-sized Barbie Dream Houses and interactive installations. "Barbie" became one of the highest-grossing films of the year and sparked numerous viral trends and memes.

2. **"Oppenheimer" - Director:** Christopher Nolan

Oppenheimer is based on the biographical drama about J. Robert Oppenheimer, the physicist who played a key role in the development of the atomic bomb. Director Nolan and the team conducted extensive research and consulted with historians to ensure historical accuracy, though some dramatic liberties were taken for cinematic effect.

Cillian Murphy: Starred as J. Robert Oppenheimer. His portrayal was noted for its depth and intensity, capturing the internal conflicts and ethical dilemmas faced by Oppenheimer. The film featured a stellar ensemble cast, including Emily Blunt, Matt Damon, Robert Downey Jr., and Florence Pugh, each contributing significantly to the narrative with their strong performances.

Trivia: This biographical drama about J. Robert Oppenheimer, the "father of the atomic bomb," was noted for its IMAX film format and use of practical effects. It garnered critical acclaim and was praised for its intense storytelling and historical accuracy.

3. "Mission: Impossible - Dead Reckoning Part One" - Director: Christopher McQuarrie

Mission: Impossible – Dead Reckoning Part One, released in 2023, continues the high-octane action franchise with Tom Cruise reprising his role as Ethan Hunt. Tom Cruise, known for performing his own stunts, took on several daring and dangerous sequences in the film. One of the most talked-about stunts was a high-altitude parachute jump and a thrilling motorcycle chase, showcasing Cruise's commitment to authenticity and excitement.

"Dead Reckoning Part One" is the first half of a two-part narrative. The decision to split the story into two parts allowed for a more elaborate and intricate plot, setting up the conclusion for the next installment.

Trivia: Several beloved characters from previous films returned, including Simon Pegg as Benji Dunn and Ving Rhames as Luther Stickell. Their return added continuity and depth to the ongoing story.

STREAMING HITS

1. **"The Last of Us"** - HBO Max

"The Last of Us," which premiered as a television series on HBO Max in January 2023, is based on the critically acclaimed video game of the same name developed by Naughty Dog. The show was created by Neil Druckmann, who co-wrote and co-directed the original game, and Craig Mazin, known for his work on "Chernobyl." Their collaboration ensured a faithful adaptation while expanding the story for television.

The series introduced new elements and expanded upon the game's story, adding depth to the world-building and character arcs. This included exploring backstories and side characters not fully detailed in the game.

Trivia: Adapted from the popular video game, this series became a major hit for its faithful representation of the game's post-apocalyptic world and strong performances by Pedro Pascal and Bella Ramsey. It sparked conversations about video game adaptations in television.

2. **"Wednesday"** - Netflix

The "Wednesday" TV series, which premiered on Netflix in November 2022, centers on Wednesday Addams from "The Addams Family." Director Tim Burton, known for his distinctive style and previous works like "Beetlejuice" and "Edward

Scissorhands," made his directorial debut in television with "Wednesday." His vision brought a unique, darkly whimsical touch to the series.

The series follows Wednesday as a student at Nevermore Academy, a school for outcasts and supernatural beings. This setting provides a fresh take on the character and introduces new elements to the Addams Family universe.It also delves into themes of identity, family, and self-discovery while maintaining the humor and dark tone associated with the Addams Family. It offers a deeper exploration of Wednesday's character and her place in the world.

Trivia: The show, focusing on Wednesday Addams from "The Addams Family," was praised for its unique take on the character, blending mystery, horror, and dark humor. It quickly became one of Netflix's most-watched shows.

3. **"Succession" (Season 4)** - HBO Max

"Succession" Season 4, which premiered in 2023, is the final season of the critically acclaimed HBO drama series created by Jesse Armstrong. The show focuses on the power struggles within the Roy family, who own a global media conglomerate. The season continues to explore themes of power, betrayal, and family dynamics as the Roy siblings vie for control of the company. The stakes are heightened as the series heads toward its conclusion.

Season 4 featured notable guest stars, adding depth and intrigue to the story. These guest appearances often played crucial roles in the unfolding drama and power struggles. The season provided resolution to long-running storylines, addressing the fates of key characters and the ultimate outcome of the Roy family's power struggles.

Trivia: The final season of this critically acclaimed drama was highly anticipated and did not disappoint. It concluded with a dramatic and controversial ending that sparked widespread debate among fans and critics.

SURPRISE INDIE SUCCESSES OF 2023

https://uproxx.com/entertainment/

1. **"Everything Everywhere All at Once" - Director:** Daniel Kwan and Daniel Scheinert

The story centers on a laundromat owner who discovers she must connect with parallel universe versions of herself to save the multiverse. The film's creative take on the multiverse concept is a major highlight. Michelle Yeoh stars as Evelyn Wang, the film's protagonist. Her performance was widely praised for its range and depth, showcasing her versatility as an actress. The role allowed Yeoh to explore a wide spectrum of emotions and actions.

The film is known for its distinctive visual style, which includes a mix of practical effects, animation, and creative editing techniques. The use of low-budget special effects combined with inventive cinematography contributes to its unique look. The film generated significant discussion and fan engagement due to its complex narrative and imaginative execution. It sparked conversations about its themes and interpretations, contributing to its popularity.

Trivia: Although released in 2022, the film continued to gain momentum into 2023, winning several awards and receiving widespread acclaim for its inventive storytelling and multiverse concept.

2. "Past Lives" - Director: Celine Song

"Past Lives," a romantic drama directed by Celine Song and released in 2023, explores themes of love, memory, and destiny through the lens of a reunion between childhood friends. Celine Song drew on her own experiences and cultural background to craft the story, infusing the film with authentic emotions and relatable themes about love and destiny.

The film received praise at several film festivals, including Sundance, where it was recognized for its emotional storytelling and innovative approach. It garnered a strong positive response from both critics and audiences. The film's portrayal of love and memory resonated deeply with audiences, prompting discussions about relationships and the impact of personal history on one's life path.

Trivia: This romantic drama about two childhood friends reconnecting after years apart was praised for its heartfelt storytelling and nuanced performances. It became a festival favorite and gained significant attention for its emotional depth.

3. "A Good Person" - Director: Zach Braff

"A Good Person," directed by Zach Braff and released in 2023, is a drama that delves into themes of forgiveness, redemption, and personal growth. The film marks Zach Braff's return to directing and writing since his previous feature, "Going in Style." Known for his work on "Garden State" and "Scrubs," Braff's involvement brings a personal touch to the film's storytelling.

"A Good Person" explores themes of redemption and personal growth as the protagonist grapples with her past mistakes and seeks to make amends. The story centers on the challenges of forgiveness and the journey towards self-improvement. The film's characters undergo significant emotional growth and development. This focus on character arcs adds depth to the narrative and allows for a more engaging and immersive experience.

Trivia: Known for its exploration of personal redemption and healing, this film received positive reviews for its strong performances and relatable themes. It stood out among indie releases for its compelling narrative and character development.

4. **"Flora and Son" - Director:** John Carney

This 2023 film is a musical drama that explores themes of family, music, and personal transformation. Known for his work on musical films such as "Once" and "Sing Street," John Carney returns with "Flora and Son," bringing his signature touch to the film's music and emotional storytelling.

Eve Hewson stars as Flora, the central character. Her performance has been praised for its emotional depth and her ability to connect with the film's themes of personal growth and family dynamics. The film's characters undergo significant development, particularly Flora as she navigates her personal challenges and relationships. This focus on character arcs adds depth to the narrative.

Trivia: A musical drama about a single mother and her son, this film gained attention for its catchy music and uplifting story. It was a surprise hit at film festivals and garnered a strong following due to its charm and originality.

These highlights showcase a range of entertainment options

from blockbuster spectacles to indie gems, reflecting the diverse tastes and trends in 2023's media landscape.

MUSIC & CELEBRITIES

2023 was a vibrant year in music, with a mix of chart-topping songs, viral moments, and emerging stars making waves. Here are some fun and interesting facts about the year's musical landscape:

Chart-Topping Songs
https://www.billboard.com/

"Flowers" by Miley Cyrus: Its catchy melody and empowering lyrics helped it become a global hit and an anthem for self-empowerment. "Flowers" debuted at number one on the Billboard Hot 100 and remained there for multiple weeks, solidifying its position as one of the biggest hits of 2023. The track was inspired by Miley's personal experiences and reflects a sense of self-discovery and personal growth. It has been seen as a response to her past relationships and a celebration of self-worth. The song became a viral hit on social media platforms, with users creating memes and videos set to the track. Its catchy chorus and empowering message contributed to its widespread appeal.

"Kill Bill" by SZA: The song is featured on SZA's highly anticipated album *SOS*, which was praised for its diverse range of sounds and introspective lyrics. The album's success further boosted the popularity of "Kill Bill." The song achieved significant chart success, reaching the top of the Billboard Hot 100 and staying there for several weeks. It was one of the standout tracks from SZA's *SOS* album. The song's title and some of its themes are a nod to Quentin Tarantino's *Kill Bill* film series. This reference adds an additional layer of cultural context and intrigue to the track.

VIRAL MOMENTS

TikTok Trends:

https://newsroom.tiktok.com/en-us/whats-next-2023-trend-report?lang=en

Dance challenges remained a staple of TikTok, with users creating and participating in choreographed routines to popular songs. Songs like "Good Good" by Usher, Summer Walker, and Lil Jon became viral sensations on TikTok, driving their popularity and chart success through viral dance challenges and memes. The phrase "it's giving" became popular for describing the aesthetic or vibe of a person, place, or thing. TikTok users used this phrase to showcase various fashion styles, home decor, and personal looks. TikTok also continued to influence fashion and beauty trends, with users showcasing makeup tutorials, fashion hauls, and style transformations. Trends included retro-inspired looks and innovative makeup techniques.

AI-Created Music: AI-generated music started making waves, with tools like OpenAI's Jukebox and other platforms creating songs that went viral. This trend sparked discussions about the future of music creation. Some musicians and producers began collaborating with AI to create music. Artists used AI-generated melodies and beats as a starting point, incorporating their own creativity and style to produce unique tracks.

BIGGEST STARS

Taylor Swift's Eras Tour: Taylor Swift's Eras Tour became one of the most talked-about events of the year, with record-breaking attendance and high demand for tickets. The tour celebrated her extensive discography and captivated fans worldwide. The tour broke records for ticket sales, with millions of fans vying for tickets. The high demand led to some of the biggest sales numbers in concert history and created a buzz around the tour. Taylor Swift incorporated interactive elements into her shows, such as fan voting on setlists and interactive social media campaigns, enhancing the connection between her and her audience.

Bad Bunny: Continuing his global success, Bad Bunny solidified his position as a leading artist in Latin music. His album *Un Verano Sin Ti* remained influential, and he made headlines with notable collaborations and performances. In 2023, several singles from *Un Verano Sin Ti* continued to dominate the charts. Songs like "Tití Me Preguntó" and "Me Porto Bonito" were particularly popular, showcasing Bad Bunny's continued appeal. Bad Bunny won the Grammy Award for Best Música Urbana Album, marking another major achievement in his career. This win highlighted his influence and success in the music industry.

RECORD-BREAKING ACHIEVEMENTS

Beyoncé's Renaissance: Beyoncé's *Renaissance* album received critical acclaim and commercial success. The album is heavily influenced by house and disco genres, showcasing a celebration of dance and electronic music. Beyoncé's exploration into these genres provides a fresh sonic experience that diverges from her previous work. The album's innovative sound and themes of self-expression and liberation were widely celebrated.

Ed Sheeran's Record: Ed Sheeran set new records with his album *Subtract,* which received widespread praise and charted globally. Described as one of his most vulnerable albums, "Subtract" explores themes of fear, depression, and anxiety. It represents the final installment in Sheeran's series of mathematically titled albums, following "+," "x," and "Ã·. His songwriting prowess and ability to connect with audiences continued to shine.

EMERGING ARTISTS

PinkPantheress: This UK artist gained significant attention in 2023 with her blend of pop and alternative sounds. PinkPantheress first gained attention on TikTok in 2021 with her catchy, short songs that resonated with the platform's audience. She continued to use TikTok effectively, regularly releasing snippets of new music that quickly went viral, keeping her at the forefront of internet music culture. Her tracks became viral hits and established her as a rising star in the music industry.

GloRilla: GloRilla made waves with her energetic and impactful music. Her breakout hit "F.N.F. (Let's Go)" earned her a spot on the charts and success of the song has helped establish GloRilla as a significant new voice in rap, noted for her unique style and energetic performances. The song's popularity was significantly boosted by TikTok, where users created numerous videos featuring dances and challenges set to its music.

GENRE TRENDS

Hyperpop continued to gain popularity, with artists like **100 gecs** and **Charli XCX** leading the charge. What once started as a niche internet genre began to cross over into the mainstream in 2023. Artists who were associated with hyperpop gained significant radio play and were featured on major music festival lineups, which introduced the genre to a broader audience. The genre's experimental and genre-blending nature attracted a dedicated following.

Disco experienced a significant revival in 2023, with artists incorporating classic disco elements into contemporary music. This trend included groovy basslines, shimmering strings, and catchy hooks reminiscent of the 70's Disco Era. Tracks that combined these elements with modern pop production found their way into mainstream charts. Several artists released albums that paid homage to the disco era while blending it with contemporary sounds. For example, **Dua Lipa's** "Future Nostalgia" continued to influence the genre with its disco-pop fusion, and other artists followed suit, creating entire albums centered around disco-inspired themes.

MUSIC FESTIVALS AND EVENTS

Major music festivals like Coachella and Glastonbury saw record attendance and memorable performances from top artists. These events served as major cultural touchpoints in the music scene. Coachella 2023 set a new attendance record, with over 250,000 people flocking to the Empire Polo Club in Indio, California, across both weekends. The festival's popularity continues to grow, attracting fans from all over the world. Coachella is as much about fashion as it is about music. 2023 saw a mix of retro styles, bold colors, and sustainable fashion choices. The festival's grounds became a runway for influencers and fashionistas.

Elton John headlined Glastonbury 2023 as part of his farewell tour, delivering a historic performance that was both emotional and electrifying. It was one of the most talked-about sets of the festival. True to Glastonbury tradition, 2023 saw its fair share of rain, turning parts of the festival grounds into muddy fields. Rather than dampening spirits, the mud added to the experience, with festival-goers embracing the elements. Glastonbury 2023 continued to create legendary moments in music history, with several artists debuting new music or collaborating live on stage. These moments often became viral online, adding to the festival's storied legacy.

SOCIAL MEDIA INFLUENCE

Charli D'Amelio remained one of TikTok's biggest stars, known for her dance videos and engaging content. Her influence extended beyond TikTok, with successful collaborations and a strong presence on other social media platforms.

Addison Rae continued to be a prominent figure on TikTok, Instagram, and YouTube. Her popularity was bolstered by her acting career and music releases, making her a versatile influencer.

Known for his creative and mind-bending "magic" videos, **Zach King** maintained his popularity in 2023 with visually captivating content that blends magic and storytelling.

Emma Chamberlain remained influential with her YouTube vlogs and personal brand. She continued to engage her audience with authentic content and was involved in various fashion and lifestyle projects.

Bella Poarch gained attention with her viral lip-sync videos and music releases. Her unique content and distinctive style kept her in the spotlight throughout 2023.

Arielle Charnas, known for her fashion and lifestyle content, continued to influence trends and collaborate with brands, maintaining her status as a prominent fashion influencer.

2023 was a dynamic year in music, marked by diverse sounds, innovative trends, and the continued influence of digital platforms on how music is created, shared, and enjoyed. This shows how the music industry in 2023 is both preserving its traditional roots and embracing new technologies and business models. For more detailed insights, you can explore comprehensive reports and articles from industry leaders and analysts, which are available on websites like Billboard and Music Business Worldwide. These resources provide in-depth coverage of the latest developments and forecasts for the future of the industry.

MEMES AND INTERNET TRENDS

"NPC streaming" became a viral trend on platforms like TikTok, where creators acted like non-playable characters (NPCs) from video games. They would repeat specific phrases or actions in response to virtual gifts from viewers, mimicking the awkward, repetitive behavior of NPCs in games. It led to some bizarre and hilarious live streams.

The **de-influencing** trend flipped the script on traditional influencer culture, with creators advising their followers on what *not* to buy. This often included humorous takes on overhyped products and the realities behind viral items, offering a refreshing and funny perspective on consumerism.

"Rizz," short for charisma, became a popular slang term and trend. People shared videos showcasing their "rizz" or lack thereof, often in exaggerated or comedic ways, leading to a wave of funny content around flirting, dating, and charm.

The **"Couch Guy"** phenomenon, which began in 2021, continued to spark viral discussions in 2023. Internet sleuths dissected relationship dynamics in short clips, often jumping to humorous and exaggerated conclusions about what might be happening in the background.

The **"Everything Shower"** trend had people detailing their extensive and often over-the-top shower routines. While some took it seriously, others exaggerated the trend for comedic effect, listing absurd steps and products to poke fun at the idea of self-care gone overboard.

"Bare Minimum Mondays" became a viral trend where people shared their minimalist approach to starting the week. The concept was both relatable and funny, with people exaggerating how little they intended to do on Mondays as a form of self-care and rebellion against hustle culture.

The **"No Bones Day"** trend, based on the behavior of a pug named Noodle, saw a revival in 2023. The concept—where a "bones" day meant a good, energetic day and a "no bones" day meant a lazy, low-energy one—continued to amuse the internet, with many jokingly planning their days around the pug's "predictions."

"Corn Kid," a young boy who expressed his love for corn in a viral interview, became a meme sensation. His earnest and joyful declaration, "I can't imagine a more beautiful thing!" was remixed and shared widely, bringing smiles and laughs across the internet.

CHAPTER 4:

Weird and Wacky News of 2023

In a world where the news cycle is dominated by serious headlines and breaking stories, sometimes it's the strange and unusual tales that capture our attention the most. Whether it's bizarre animal antics, unexpected political developments, or unexplainable natural phenomena, these oddball headlines remind us that life is full of surprises. From mysterious sheep circles to AI politicians, the year 2023 was no exception, delivering a host of stories that left us scratching our heads, laughing out loud, and marveling at the sheer unpredictability of the world around us. Here's a look at some of the most peculiar and intriguing news stories in 2023.

In 2023, a town in Western Australia found itself overrun by emus after a long absence. The large birds, which are native to the region, wandered into the town in search of food and water due to drought conditions. The sight of these giant birds casually strolling through urban streets was both amusing and concerning for residents.

In an unexpected twist, an AI chatbot running on a platform similar to ChatGPT won a local election in a small Japanese town. The bot, designed to manage municipal tasks more efficiently, ran on a platform of transparency, promising to log all its decisions publicly. The election raised questions about the future of AI in governance and public administration.

A viral video from Inner Mongolia showed a flock of sheep walking in a perfect circle for 12 days straight without stopping. The behavior baffled scientists and observers, leading to various theories ranging from magnetic field disturbances to a simple case of "follow the leader" gone viral. The phenomenon remains unexplained.

Disneyland in California had to briefly shut down after a wild bear was spotted roaming near the park's entrance. The bear, likely attracted by the scent of food, caused a stir among visitors before being safely tranquilized and relocated. The incident led to a flurry of bear-themed merchandise and memes.

Dubai officially launched the world's first flying taxi service in 2023, with drones ferrying passengers across the city. While the concept had been in development for years, it was surreal to see flying taxis become a reality. The sight of futuristic vehicles zipping through the skies marked a milestone in urban transportation.

A message in a bottle, thrown into the ocean over a century ago, was discovered on a beach in Scotland in 2023. The note, dated 1906, was remarkably well-preserved and detailed the sender's hopes for the future. The discovery sparked widespread interest in the history of oceanic currents and the long-lost art of message-in-a-bottle communication.

A mysterious monolith, similar to those that popped up in 2020, reappeared in several locations around the world in 2023, sparking renewed speculation about their origin. The monoliths, which appeared overnight in remote areas, continued to puzzle experts and inspire conspiracy theories, despite likely being part of an elaborate global art project.

Two penguins from a local zoo somehow ended up wandering the New York City subway system in 2023, much to the surprise of commuters. The penguins, later identified as escapees from a nearby zoo, were safely returned, but not before charming the city and becoming an unexpected symbol of resilience and adventure.

UNBELIEVABLE WORLD RECORDS

2023 was a year full of jaw-dropping achievements as people around the globe pushed the boundaries of what's possible, setting some truly unbelievable world records. Here's a glimpse of some of the most astonishing feats:

LAKE SILS, Switzerland, March 14 (Reuters) - David Vencl emerged from the depths of Switzerland's Lake Sils on Tuesday after a record dive beneath the ice to a depth of more than 50 meters without a wetsuit. The 40-year-old Czech diver's record vertical plunge to 52.1 meters in a single breath follows his entry into the Guinness World Records book for swimming the length of a frozen Czech lake in 2021.

In an event that combined fun and precision, over 2,000 participants set a new record for the largest human mattress domino chain in China. The participants fell backward onto mattresses in a domino effect, with the entire chain taking several minutes to complete.

In Mexico City, over 35,000 people gathered to set the record for the largest number of people dressed as zombies. The event, part of a Halloween celebration, saw participants in elaborate zombie makeup and costumes, shambling through the streets to claim the title.

A British man set a new world record by balancing seven M&M's on top of each other, surpassing the previous record of six. The feat required incredible patience and steady hands, given the tiny size and irregular shape of the candies.

An Australian man set the record for the fastest time to eat a raw onion, consuming the pungent vegetable in just 26.15 seconds. The record attempt was as impressive as it was uncomfortable, with the man shedding tears as he powered through the challenge.

In the Netherlands, a restaurant set a new world record for the most expensive burger, selling it for €5,000 (approximately $5,600 US Dollars). The burger featured ingredients like Japanese wagyu beef, white truffle, Beluga caviar, and gold leaf, making it a meal fit for royalty.

An Indian athlete set an unusual record by spinning a basketball on a toothbrush for a staggering 1 minute and 8.15 seconds. The toothbrush was held in his mouth, showcasing incredible balance and control.

A devoted Pokémon fan in the U.S. broke the record for the largest collection of Pokémon memorabilia, amassing over 25,000 items. The collection included everything from trading cards and plush toys to rare collectibles and promotional items.

A man from Australia set a new world record by holding the plank position for an astonishing 10 hours, 5 minutes, and 42 seconds. This feat of endurance required immense core strength and mental fortitude, breaking the previous record by nearly an hour.

A Spanish performer set a new record for the most juggling catches using only his feet, achieving 128 catches in just one minute. The record was set using three balls, and the performer had to keep them in constant motion, using only his feet to catch and toss them.

These incredible records highlight the creativity, determination, and sometimes downright bizarre pursuits of people around the world. From feats of physical endurance to quirky challenges, 2023 was a year that pushed the limits of human achievement in ways that were as impressive as they were unbelievable.

QUIRKY INVENTIONS

2023 witnessed the emergence of some truly bizarre and creative inventions, showcasing the boundless imagination and ingenuity of inventors worldwide. Here are details on some of the most unusual and innovative creations that made headlines in 2023.

In a bid to improve sleep quality, a tech company unveiled a "Smart Pillow" that not only tracks your sleep patterns but also adjusts its shape and firmness throughout the night. Equipped with AI, this pillow learns your preferred sleeping positions and can warm or cool itself to help you drift off more comfortably. It even plays soothing sounds or wakes you up with gentle vibrations at the optimal time in your sleep cycle.

In an effort to combat plastic pollution, a startup introduced edible water bottles made from biodegradable seaweed-based packaging. These spherical water containers, known as "Ooho," can be consumed entirely or discarded, as they break down naturally within weeks. This eco-friendly invention has the potential to revolutionize hydration on the go, especially in outdoor events and marathons.

A sleek, minimalist pen that hovers above its base, seemingly defying gravity, became a hit in 2023. The pen uses a combination of magnetic fields to float in mid-air when placed on its stand. Not only does it serve as a functional writing instrument, but it also doubles as a mesmerizing desk accessory that intrigues anyone who sees it.

With the decline of natural bee populations posing a threat to global agriculture, 2023 saw the development of robotic bees designed to assist with pollination. These tiny, drone-like devices mimic the behavior of real bees, using advanced sensors and AI to identify and pollinate flowers. While not a replacement for natural bees, these robotic counterparts could help support crop growth in areas facing pollinator shortages.

The "No-Button Microwave." This microwave operates entirely through gesture controls, eliminating the need for buttons or dials. Users can simply wave their hand or perform specific gestures to start, stop, and adjust cooking settings. The microwave's AI interprets these gestures in real-time, offering a futuristic and hygienic way to prepare food.

In response to increasing air pollution concerns, a designer created shoes with built-in air purifiers. As the wearer walks, the movement powers tiny filters in the soles that purify the air around the feet, effectively cleaning the air one step at a time. While the concept might sound odd, it highlights innovative thinking in tackling environmental issues.

Engineers developed a fire extinguisher that uses low-frequency sound waves to put out fires. This invention works by directing a powerful blast of sound at the flames, disrupting the air and effectively starving the fire of oxygen. This sound-based extinguisher is particularly useful for small, controlled fires and could be adapted for use in various environments where traditional extinguishers are impractical.

Building on the popularity of weighted blankets, the Gravity Blanket 2.0 offers customizable weight distribution through adjustable pockets filled with microbeads. Users can fine-tune the blanket's weight and balance to match their personal preferences, providing a tailor-made solution for reducing anxiety and improving sleep.

Tired of burnt toast? A transparent toaster made waves in 2023 by allowing users to watch their bread toast to perfection. The toaster uses heat-resistant glass and advanced heating elements that let you monitor the browning process in real-time, ensuring your toast is exactly how you like it every time.

3D-printed vegan meat products became a reality in 2023, offering consumers a new way to enjoy plant-based proteins. These printers can create meat substitutes with tailored textures, flavors, and nutritional profiles, allowing for customized meals that cater to individual dietary needs and preferences. This technology not only provides an eco-friendly alternative to traditional meat but also opens up new possibilities in food innovation.

These bizarre and creative inventions from 2023 illustrate how inventors are pushing the boundaries of technology, sustainability, and everyday convenience. From AI-driven household items to eco-conscious innovations, these creations reflect the diverse and imaginative spirit of the modern age.

CHAPTER 5:

Food and Travel Trends of 2023

2023 was a year full of exciting developments in the culinary world, with food trends that reflected both a growing interest in sustainability and a love for bold, viral flavors. Here's a look at some of the hottest food trends, including plant-based innovations and viral dishes:

TOP FOOD TRENDS

Plant-based alternatives continued to dominate the food scene in 2023, but it wasn't just about burgers anymore. Companies innovated with plant-based seafood, like tuna, shrimp, and even calamari, offering consumers more sustainable options. Notably, plant-based eggs made from mung beans and chickpeas became widely popular, with their taste and texture closely mimicking real eggs.

Mushrooms were the star ingredient of 2023, celebrated for their versatility, umami flavor, and sustainability. From mushroom jerky and coffee to innovative dishes like "mushroom scallops" and "pulled mushroom" sandwiches, fungi were everywhere. Lion's mane mushrooms, in particular, gained popularity as a meat substitute, known for their meaty texture and health benefits.

Fermented foods like kimchi, kombucha, and kefir continued to grow in popularity due to their gut health benefits. In 2023, home fermentation kits became a hit, with people making their own pickles, sauerkraut, and even miso at home. Fermented honey and soy-free miso, made from chickpeas or other legumes, also became trendy as new takes on traditional flavors.

Following the viral trend of charcuterie boards, butter boards became a massive hit in 2023. The concept involved spreading softened butter across a wooden board and topping it with a variety of ingredients like edible flowers, herbs, spices, and flavored salts. Served with fresh bread, these boards became the go-to centerpiece for dinner parties and social media food photos.

2023 saw the commercial debut of lab-grown meat, also known as cultivated meat. These products, made from animal cells without the need for slaughter, started appearing in upscale restaurants and specialty stores. Chicken and beef were the first meats to hit the market, with pork and seafood not far behind. The trend reflected a growing interest in sustainable and ethical food production.

Asian cuisine continued to influence global food trends, with dishes like Korean corn dogs, Japanese soufflé pancakes, and Chinese hotpot gaining widespread popularity. 2023 also saw a surge in Asian fusion dishes, blending traditional flavors with modern twists, such as sushi tacos, ramen burgers, and Thai curry pizza.

With a focus on reducing food waste, upcycled foods became a significant trend in 2023. Companies started creating snacks and ingredients from food by-products, like chips made from leftover pulp from juicing or flour made from spent grain from breweries. This trend aligned with consumers' growing interest in sustainability and waste reduction.

TikTok continued to be a major source of food trends, with viral recipes dominating the platform. In 2023, dishes like "cloud bread," "pasta chips," and "cottage cheese ice cream" took the internet by storm. TikTok's short-form videos made it easy for home cooks to recreate these recipes, driving trends that often went viral overnight.

The "sober curious" movement grew stronger in 2023, with a rise in alcohol-free spirits and cocktails. These sophisticated, non-alcoholic beverages offered complex flavors and the experience of a cocktail without the alcohol. Bartenders got creative with ingredients like botanicals, herbs, and fermented drinks to craft delicious mocktails that appealed to a health-conscious crowd.

These food trends from 2023 highlight the evolving landscape of what we eat and how we experience food, with a focus on sustainability, creativity, and the influence of digital culture. Whether it's indulging in a viral dish or exploring the latest plant-based innovation, 2023 was a year of culinary excitement and experimentation.

MUST-VISIT DESTINATIONS

In 2023, the world of travel was full of exciting new destinations and unique attractions that captivated adventurers and culture seekers alike. Here's a roundup of some of the most interesting travel trends and standout attractions from the year.

2023 saw the beginning of more accessible space tourism, with companies like Blue Origin and SpaceX offering suborbital flights. While these trips are still pricey, they allowed a handful of lucky travelers to experience weightlessness and see Earth from space, marking the start of a new era in travel.

Underwater hotels became increasingly popular in 2023, offering guests the chance to sleep surrounded by marine life. The "Poseidon Undersea Resort" in Fiji and the "The Muraka" suite in the Maldives provided stunning views of underwater ecosystems, with rooms submerged below the ocean's surface.

AI-driven travel apps and platforms revolutionized how people planned their trips in 2023. These tools offered personalized recommendations based on user preferences, real-time updates, and even virtual travel assistants to help with bookings, making travel planning more efficient and customized.

Micro-adventures, defined as short, local getaways that offer a break from routine without the need for long-haul travel, became a trend in 2023. These included urban explorations, weekend hikes, and day trips to nearby natural wonders, catering to those looking for quick, refreshing escapes.

Cities and countries embraced the digital nomad lifestyle in 2023, offering special visas and perks for remote workers. Places like Bali, Lisbon, and Medellín became popular hubs, providing co-working spaces, vibrant communities, and affordable living options for those working while traveling.

Extreme weather phenomena became a unique attraction, with travelers seeking out destinations known for dramatic weather conditions. Popular spots included the Northern Lights in Iceland, monsoon storms in Thailand, and the Sahara Desert's extreme heat, catering to adventure seekers looking for rare weather experiences.

Food-based travel continued to grow, with culinary tours and food festivals drawing visitors from around the world. Destinations like Tokyo, Barcelona, and Mexico City became hotspots for foodies, offering diverse culinary experiences from street food tours to fine dining adventures.

Virtual reality (VR) travel experiences gained traction, allowing users to explore destinations and attractions from the comfort of their homes. VR tours of iconic landmarks, historical sites, and natural wonders offered a new way to experience travel, especially for those unable to visit in person.

Luxury treehouses and glamping sites offered a blend of comfort and nature in 2023. Destinations like the "Treehotel" in Sweden and "Under Canvas" sites across the U.S. provided upscale camping experiences with amenities such as plush beds, gourmet meals, and stunning natural settings.

Historical reenactments and immersive experiences became popular, allowing travelers to step back in time. Events like medieval fairs in Europe, Revolutionary War reenactments in the U.S., and traditional cultural festivals in Asia offered a hands-on approach to history and culture.

Floating islands and luxurious cruise experiences captured imaginations in 2023. Innovative projects like floating hotels and luxury cruise ships with onboard amenities such as spas, theaters, and gourmet dining offered unique ways to explore the world's oceans.

These travel trends and unique attractions from 2023 highlight a growing interest in both innovative experiences and sustainable, immersive adventures. Whether exploring new technologies, embracing local cultures, or seeking out extreme conditions, travelers found exciting ways to make the most of their journeys.

CHAPTER 6:

Sports and Games in 2023

2023 was a landmark year in the world of sports, marked by unforgettable moments, historic achievements, and thrilling competitions. From the dramatic finishes of global tournaments to groundbreaking performances by top athletes, the year captivated fans across the globe.

Here's a look at some of the most notable sports happenings and milestones from 2023, showcasing the excitement and drama that defined the year.

MAJOR SPORTS EVENTS

Held in France from September 8 to October 28, the Rugby World Cup saw exciting matches and surprising upsets. South Africa emerged as the champion, winning their fourth World Cup title by defeating New Zealand in the final. The tournament showcased some of the best rugby talent globally, with thrilling games and dramatic moments.

https://www.rugbyworldcup.com/2023

Held in Santiago, Chile from October 20 to November 5, the Pan American Games featured a wide range of sports and showcased athletes from across the Americas. The games included traditional sports like athletics and swimming, as well as regional favorites such as baseball and volleyball.

https://en.wikipedia.org/wiki/2023_Pan_American_Games

The Asian Games were held in Hangzhou, China, from September 23 to October 8. The event featured over 40 sports and included traditional events as well as new additions like eSports. China topped the medal table, continuing their dominance in the region's premier multi-sport event.

https://apnews.com/article/asian-games-closing-ceremony-hangzhou-china-68c2c3ce2498ec2afca500394ea9bb63

The World Athletics Championships took place in Budapest,

Hungary, from August 19 to 27. The championships featured outstanding performances, with athletes like Noah Lyles and Faith Kipyegon making headlines. Lyles, in particular, delivered an impressive performance in the 200 meters.

https://worldathletics.org/competitions/world-athletics-championships/world-athletics-championships-budapest-2023-7138987

The Formula 1 season saw Max Verstappen of Red Bull Racing dominating the championship, securing his third consecutive World Drivers' Championship. The season was notable for its competitive races and technological innovations, with Red Bull Racing showing impressive performance across the circuit.

https://www.formula1.com/en/latest/article/f1-announces-24-race-calendar-for-2023.7oNRaq4kZ2bwTAmL7r6dqg

The NBA Finals in June 2023 featured the Denver Nuggets and the Miami Heat. The Nuggets secured their first-ever NBA Championship, led by Finals MVP Nikola Jokić. The series was marked by thrilling games and high-level performances from both teams.
https://www.nba.com/playoffs/2023/the-finals

Wimbledon, held from June 26 to July 9, saw notable victories in the tennis world. Carlos Alcaraz won the men's singles title, continuing his rise as one of the sport's young stars. In the women's singles, Markéta Vondroušová claimed the title, highlighting her impressive talent on grass courts.
https://www.cnn.com/2023/07/15/sport/wimbledon-mens-final-novak-djokovic-carlos-alcaraz-spt-intl/index.html
https://www.abc.net.au/news/2023-07-16/wimbledon-final-ladies-ons-jabeur-mark%C3%A9ta-vondrou%C5%A1ov%C3%A1/102606716

The World Snooker Championship, held in Sheffield, England, saw a thrilling final with Ronnie O'Sullivan clinching his seventh world title. O'Sullivan's performance was widely praised, reaffirming his status as one of the greatest snooker players of all time.
https://www.bbc.com/sport/snooker/65055658

The X Games, known for extreme sports, took place in Los Angeles from July 13 to 16. The event featured high-flying performances in skateboarding, BMX, and motocross. Athletes showcased incredible skills and daring feats, making it a highlight for fans of extreme sports.
https://www.xgames.com/events/x-games-california-2023

Various sports saw record-breaking performances in 2023. For example, swimmer Katie Ledecky set new records in long-distance freestyle events, and cyclist Tadej Pogačar achieved remarkable results in major cycling tours, further solidifying his place as a top competitor.

The UEFA Champions League final was held on June 10, with Manchester City winning their first European title by defeating Inter Milan. The victory was celebrated as a historic moment for Manchester City, highlighting their rise in European football.
https://en.wikipedia.org/
wiki/2023_UEFA_Champions_League_final

As 2023 came to a close, it left behind a legacy of extraordinary achievements, unforgettable moments, and inspiring performances. From thrilling finals and historic victories to groundbreaking records and emerging talents, the year showcased the relentless passion and excitement that define the world of sports. These events not only celebrated athletic excellence but also captured the imagination of fans worldwide, making 2023 a memorable chapter in the ongoing saga of sports history.

RECORD-BREAKING PERFORMANCES

In 2023, the world of sports witnessed a series of remarkable feats as athletes pushed the limits of human performance and set new records across a range of disciplines. From the pool to the track, and from the racecourse to the arena, these exceptional achievements not only captivated fans but also redefined the standards of excellence in their respective sports. Here's a look at some of the most standout record-breaking moments of the year.

Katie Ledecky continued her dominance in long-distance swimming by setting new world records in the 800m and 1500m freestyle events. Her performances at the World Swimming Championships in Fukuoka, Japan, showcased her exceptional endurance and skill, reinforcing her status as one of the greatest swimmers of all time.

Max Verstappen set a new record for the most consecutive wins in a single Formula 1 season. His impressive performance throughout the 2023 season led him to secure his third consecutive World Drivers' Championship, further solidifying his place among the sport's elite drivers.

Tadej Pogačar made history by becoming the first rider to win the Tour de France in consecutive years with the same team, UAE Team Emirates. His exceptional climbing and time-trialing skills led him to a dominant performance, breaking several stage records along the way.

Armand Duplantis set a new world record in the pole vault at the World Athletics Championships in Budapest, clearing a height of 6.23 meters. His remarkable feat continued to push the boundaries of the sport and established him as the premier pole vaulter in history.

Sifan Hassan set a new world record in the women's 10,000 meters and achieved a remarkable double win at the World Athletics Championships in Budapest by also winning the 5,000 meters. Her performances demonstrated exceptional versatility and endurance.

Although **Tom Brady** retired from professional football in early 2023, he set new records over his career that continued to influence the sport. Notably, he holds the record for the most career touchdown passes and Super Bowl victories, cementing his legacy as one of the greatest quarterbacks of all time.

Elaine Thompson-Herah set new records in the 100 meters and 200 meters sprint events at the Diamond League meetings. Her lightning-fast times showcased her remarkable speed and consistency on the track.

Jude Bellingham set records as the youngest player to score in multiple World Cup matches. His performances at the 2022 World Cup and continued excellence in 2023 highlighted his talent and potential as one of football's rising stars.

Sha'Carri Richardson set a new American record in the 100 meters during the U.S. Track and Field Championships. Her explosive speed and competitive spirit marked her as a key athlete in the sprinting world.

Even though **Serena Williams** retired in 2022, her influence in 2023 was still felt as records she set, such as the most Grand Slam titles in the Open Era, continued to be celebrated and analyzed by sports enthusiasts.

The incredible feats achieved by athletes across the globe in 2023, underscored the relentless pursuit of greatness and the evolution of sports. These new records not only celebrated individual brilliance and determination but also inspired countless others to reach for their own heights. With each record set, the boundaries of what's possible in sports were pushed further, leaving an indelible mark on the year and setting the stage for future excellence.

CONCLUSION

Festivals like Coachella and Glastonbury continued to be cultural highlights, while unique events like the Chinchilla Melon Festival and Sechseläuten showcased the world's diverse cultural traditions and quirky celebrations. Breakthroughs in AI, such as AI-generated music and advancements in robotics, transformed various industries and daily life, pushing the boundaries of what technology can achieve. Major releases like "Barbie," "Oppenheimer," and "Mission Impossible: Dead Reckoning Part 1" captivated audiences. The year saw a mix of high-profile films and critically acclaimed TV shows, showcasing a diverse range of storytelling and cinematic experiences.

The Rugby World Cup, Women's World Cup, and other significant sporting events delivered thrilling matches and historic victories, marking 2023 as a year of sports excellence and memorable moments. Athletes set new records across various sports, including Katie Ledecky in swimming, Max Verstappen in Formula 1, and Armand Duplantis in pole vaulting. These achievements highlighted the year as one of extraordinary athletic excellence. The year also saw a surge in interest for space tourism, underwater hotels, and eco-lodges, reflecting a growing desire for unique and immersive travel experiences. Overall, 2023 was defined by a blend of remarkable achievements, creative breakthroughs, and cultural milestones that left a lasting impact on entertainment, technology, sports, and beyond.

As we reflect on the remarkable moments of 2023, it's clear that the year set new standards and inspired fresh possibilities across various fields. From groundbreaking sports achievements and innovative technological advancements to vibrant cultural celebrations and memorable entertainment, 2023 was a testament to human creativity and resilience. Looking ahead, these milestones not only provide a foundation for future excellence but also spark excitement for the new horizons yet to be explored. As we move forward, the lessons and inspirations from this year will undoubtedly shape the next era of progress and innovation.

BONUS SECTION:
2023 Facts Quiz

1. Sports Achievements

Question 1: Who set a new world record in the pole vault at the 2023 World Athletics Championships?

A) Mondo Duplantis

B) Armand Duplantis

C) Sam Kendricks

D) Chris Nilsen

Question 2: Which team won the 2023 FIFA Women's World Cup?

A) United States

B) Spain

C) England

D) Australia

Question 3: Which driver secured their third consecutive World Drivers' Championship in Formula 1 in 2023?

A) Lewis Hamilton

B) Max Verstappen

C) Charles Leclerc

D) George Russell

2. Entertainment

Question 4: Which 2023 film directed by Greta Gerwig received widespread attention for its innovative take on a classic toy character?

A) "Oppenheimer"

B) "Flora and Son"

C) "Barbie"

D) "Past Lives"

Question 5: Which 2023 TV series, set in a post-apocalyptic world, received widespread acclaim for its adaptation of a popular video game?

A) "The Bear"

B) "The Last of Us"

C) "Succession"

D) "Wednesday"

Question 6: Which artist released the hit single "Flowers" in 2023?

A) Ariana Grande

B) Miley Cyrus

C) Taylor Swift

D) SZA

3. Technology

Question 7: What was the name of the AI-powered home robot released by Amazon in 2023?

A) Astro

B) Echo

C) Alexa

D) Echo Show

Question 8: Which company's 2023 product featured a smart urine analysis device for home health monitoring?

A) Withings

B) Fitbit

C) Apple

D) Garmin

Question 9: What was the name of the advanced portable power station released by Anker in 2023?

A) PowerCore 2000

B) PowerHouse 757

C) PowerPack 3000

D) PowerBoost 1000

4. Cultural Events

Question 10: What unique festival in Switzerland is celebrated by burning an effigy of a snowman?

A) Sechseläuten

B) Fête de la Musique

C) La Tomatina

D) Bastille Day

Question 11: The "Chinchilla Melon Festival" takes place in which country?

A) Australia

B) Spain

C) Japan

D) Mexico

Question 12: The "Naadam Festival" is celebrated in which country?

A) Mongolia

B) India

C) Thailand

D) Korea

5. Viral Moments and Trends

Question 13: In 2023, which dance-pop artist's album was heavily influenced by 70s disco sounds?

A) Dua Lipa

B) Lizzo

C) The Weeknd

D) SZA

Question 14: Which 2023 trend involved virtual experiences of travel and cultural events?

A) Virtual Reality Travel

B) Digital Nomad Hotspots

C) AI Travel Planning

D) Extreme Weather Tourism

Question 15: What viral social media trend involved creating short, catchy videos using a specific song?

A) Dance Challenges

B) Recipe Hacks

C) DIY Projects

D) Reaction Videos

Answers:

1. B) Armand Duplantis
2. B) Spain
3. B) Max Verstappen
4. C) "Barbie"
5. B) "The Last of Us"
6. B) Miley Cyrus
7. A) Astro
8. A) Withings
9. B) PowerHouse 757
10. A) Sechseläuten
11. A) Australia
12. A) Mongolia
13. A) Dua Lipa
14. A) Virtual Reality Travel

15. A) Dance Challenges

www.ingramcontent.com/pod-product-compliance
Lightning Source LLC
Chambersburg PA
CBHW071008250726
48653CB00005B/1561